Teaching Pupils with Severe Learning Difficulties

for Philip

Teaching Pupils with Severe Learning Difficulties: Practical Approaches

Edited by
Christina Tilstone

David Fulton Publishers
London

David Fulton Publishers Ltd
2 Barbon Close, London WC1N 3JX

First published in Great Britain by
David Fulton Publishers 1991

Reprinted 1995

Note: The right of the authors to be identified as the authors of their work has been asserted by them in accordance with the Copyright, Designs and Patents Act 1988.

British Library Cataloguing in Publication Data

Teaching pupils with severe learning difficulties:
  practical approaches.
  1. Tilstone, Christina
  371.92660941

ISBN 1-85346-171-7

Typeset by Chapterhouse, Formby, L37 3PX
Printed in Great Britain by
BPC Wheaton Ltd, Exeter.

Contents

Contributors

SUDARSHAN ABROL	Headteacher, Mayfield School, Birmingham
BETTY COWLEY	Parent
BARRY CARPENTER	Inspector (Special Educational Needs) Solihull LEA
ROBERT DOLTON	Parent
PROFESSOR RONALD GULLIFORD	Emeritus Professor, The University of Birmingham
PENNY LACEY	Lecturer in Severe Learning Difficulties, The University of Birmingham
SYLVIA LINDOE	General Adviser (Special Educational Needs) Leicestershire LEA
JULIE MOORE	Primary Inspector, London Borough of Barking and Dagenham
DR. JOGINDER PHULL	Parent
DR. BERYL SMITH	Department of Psychiatry, The University of Birmingham
FRANK STEEL	Headteacher, Rosehill School, Worcester
CHRISTINA TILSTONE	Lecturer in Severe Learning Difficulties, The University of Birmingham
JOHN VISSER	Principal Lecturer in Special Education, The University of Birmingham and Newman and Westhill Colleges
ELIZABETH YATES	Teacher, Mary Elliot School, Walsall
PROFESSOR FRANCES YOUNG	Parent

Acknowledgements

I wish to thank:
Brownie Davis, Jeremy Fathers, Mary Harrison, Rob Jeffcoat, Clare
Jones, Janine Kirby, Penny Lacey, Kathryn O'Leary, Steven Parker,
Beryl Smith, Frank Steel, John Visser, Veronica Whinney and Oliver
Wootton for their careful and critical reading of individual chapters
and for their valuable comments and suggestions. Any shortcomings
or inaccuracies, however, must be my responsibility.

The teachers on the part-time B.Phil. (Severe Learning Difficulties)
Course, University of Birmingham, for their continuing interest, their
enthusiasms and their valuable help.

The pupils who contributed to Chapter 3.

Jon Booth and Robert Charlesworth for their help with
illustrations.

Rosemary Siddles for her advice during the initial stages in the
planning of this book.

Finally, Sue Ayres who typed the whole of the manuscript and who
responded with good humour and enthusiasm to all my demands and
to 'phone calls at 'unsociable hours'!

Foreword

In a poem by Browning, voicing the thoughts of the painter Andrea del Sarto, the latter is represented as saying 'A man's reach should exceed his grasp, or what's a Heaven for?'. I have always taken this to mean that we should not rest content with what we have achieved but should always be seeking the next stage to perfection – an attitude which could well be said to characterize those who have been at the forefront of innovation and development in the education of pupils with severe difficulties in learning.

There would be general agreement that the development of education for this group of pupils has been very successful and the expectations of teachers have increased significantly. The curricular experiences offered have broadened both in terms of content and methods, and many special schools have been outward-looking in initiating cooperative activities and schemes of integration with mainstream schools. There are so many aspects of their task: developing and evaluating the whole curriculum, of which the National Curriculum is now an important part; teaching groups and individuals; managing the classroom; coordinating the work of multidisciplinary teams and working with parents (to name but a few!) that they might say with Andrea del Sarto in the poem:

> 'Had I been but two, another and myself,
> Our head would have o'erlooked the world'.

Perhaps Heads do that anyway!

These developments form Part 2 of the book and the chapters have been written by practitioners who have worked together either in and between schools, or in teacher education or advisory work.

I was glad to see that Part 1 of the book starts with an historical review. I am sure that one cannot fully understand the present without some understanding of the past. There is also a sense of identification with those who had the understanding that something needed to be done and the spirit to start doing it.

Even more valuable is the opportunity to empathize with parents and families, for without them we cannot truly understand the school's role nor some of the fuller meanings of 'special education'. For it is not just a special kind of teaching concerned only with pupils; it is unlikely to be complete without a genuine partnership with parents.

Ron Gulliford
August 1991

Preface

This book was written for teachers in mainstream and special schools who are involved in the education of pupils with severe learning difficulties. It aims to provide a comprehensive investigation of the needs of these pupils; to encourage teachers to recognize the relevance of their present skills and to encourage them to devise appropriate strategies in new and challenging contexts. Consideration is also given to essentially practical approaches to collaboration within a multi-disciplinary framework, and to the management of learning environments. The chapters on curriculum design and assessment take into account the requirements of the National Curriculum.

Sections on the social contextualization of special education consider the views of parents and pupils; the dual discrimination often suffered by pupils with severe learning difficulties from ethnic and cultural minorities; and the problems of bringing about changes in social attitudes. At a time of radical reforms it is necessary to consider in an historical overview the sweeping changes made during the present century. History might appear to be solely concerned with the past but it does enable us to contextualize current developments. 1991 marks the twentieth anniversary of the transfer from Health into Education of children with severe learning difficulties, but there is still much to be done for pupils, parents and teachers.

It is not without significance that this book is being published at a time when Specialist Initial Teacher Training (Severe Learning Difficulties) Courses have ended and new approaches to in-service training are being devised. It is hoped, therefore, that each chapter will stimulate discussions between all professionals concerned with special education.

Throughout, the terms 'she' for the teacher and 'he' for the pupil are used. No sexist implications are intended.

Christina Tilstone
Birmingham
August 1991

PART ONE

PART ONE

CHAPTER 1

Historical Review

Christina Tilstone

The Warnock Report of 1978 estimated that approximately 20 per cent of school-age children have special educational needs which, at some time during their school career, may require additional resources. Approximately 2 per cent of these children have severe physical, intellectual, or emotional difficulties and, for the last 20 years, have usually received their education in special schools or units. This book is concerned with the education of those pupils whose intellectual, emotional, and social problems are so great that they are considered to have 'severe difficulties in learning'.

A major complication in outlining the historical development of attitudes and educational provision for pupils with severe learning difficulties is the changing terminology. Not only were such children known as mentally handicapped, but as 'idiots and imbeciles', 'mentally defective', 'severely subnormal', 'severely retarded,' and 'educationally subnormal'. Today such labelling is counterproductive in educational contexts.

Wood and Shears (1986) suggest that the terminology itself can be handicapping and that labels similar to 'mental handicap' imply that those categorized are fundamentally different from their fellows. Pupils with severe learning difficulties are not part of a discrete group unless society makes them so. In subsequent chapters attempts have been made to avoid terms which are emotive or which can lead to inaccurate generalizations but in this chapter, when referring to a particular historical period, it has often been necessary to use the contemporaneous phraseology.

In the past, there were difficulties in clarifying the distinctions between mental illness and mental handicap. Roberts (1960) suggests that the difference between being mentally ill and being mentally handicapped

> is rather like the difference between falling on a frosty pavement and breaking your leg in two places and being born with one leg shorter than the other. In the first case, with any luck, you can hope to be as good as new before too long, in the second you will walk lame for the rest of your life (p. 18).

The extent to which a child 'will walk lame' thoughout life depends on early detection, assessment, and careful intervention. It also depends on his social and physical environment (Fraser, 1980). Past attitudes to handicap may still prevail, and the teacher by the very nature of her profession is in a key position to challenge and modify histori-cally-fixed perceptions. Consequently, pupils may be helped not only to take their rightful place in the community, but to contribute to a society which in the past has rejected them.

In order to teach pupils with severe learning difficulties effectively, it is necessary to recognize the major historical influence on their education and management. Hewett and Forness (1974) argue that there are four major historical pressures on the treatment of the handicapped. They list them as:

- the need for survival;
- the force of superstition;
- the findings of science;
- and the desire to be of service.

The last encompasses the care, humane treatment, and social acceptance of the handicapped. Although Hewett and Forness regard them as landmarks in each period of history, they can be interpreted as separate influences which reflect historical trends and determine current practices in special education.

The need for survival

Most primitive societies were forced to adopt the law of the 'survival of the fittest'. A child's ability to contribute to society, and consequently his or her value, became obvious at an early age and thus infanticide was the fate of the weak and deformed. In some societies (ancient Sparta for example) there were deliberate attempts to breed strong stock as an insurance against invaders. In such situations children were seen as possessions of the state, and those not passing the rigorous physical examinations were left to die through exposure. The ancient Greeks, the Romans, and the Nazis in the 1930s, were concerned not only to develop a strong army, but also to purify the race. The handicapped were seen as a burden and a dilution, and were eliminated.

Towards the end of the nineteenth century, the Eugenics movement, led by Sir Francis Galton warned of the dangers of national degeneracy and argued that a defective mother would inevitably produce defective children. Although there was no attempt to 'eliminate' the mother herself she was 'disposed of' along with her children by placing her in an isolated asylum. Tredgold and Soddy (1956), whose text book on mental deficiency became a standard text for the medical and caring professions until the 1960s, wrote of Galton:

> It is a reasonable hope that, by the study and application of these principles, we shall find the antidote to degeneracy and the true road to racial progress (p. 405).

Consequently low-grade, feeble-minded people were placed in large colonies, often in rural areas, where their lives and sexual relationships could be controlled (Cole, 1989). This segregation of mentally defective adults and their children as a possible danger to society largely contributed to the stigma often attached to special schools today.

The process of natural selection, however, meant that a severely handicapped baby was less likely than the majority of infants to endure the traumas of birth and early childhood. Recent medical advances have greatly improved the chances of prevention and detection, although it has been known for some doctors to withhold medical intervention and to allow babies to die. In 1981 Dr Leonard Arthur, a consultant paediatrician, was acquitted of taking active steps to end the life of a baby with Down's syndrome. Although Dr Arthur was found not guilty of murder, the trial revealed the poor public understanding of the individual value and social worth of children with this syndrome.

The force of superstition

Superstition and irrational fears have also been factors in shaping attitudes to the handicapped. The ancient Athenians, like the Spartans, used death by exposure to rid themselves of the handicapped, but their motivation was a fear of the unknown or a particular interpretation of religious beliefs. The advent of Christianity led to more compassionate attitudes and the New Testament contains a range of references to the handicapped; for instance:

> When even was come, they brought unto him many that were possessed with devils: and he cast out the spirits with his word and healed all that were sick (Matthew VIII.16).

Consequently, the earliest recorded attempts to provide help for the handicapped were initiated by Christians. Enlightened and humane responses were, however, often negated by Church-led attacks on the ground of heresy. With few exceptions, the mentally handicapped were regarded as witches and sorcerers and were persecuted and ridiculed as their handicaps were thought to be the result of their sins, their wanton behaviour or the sins of their fathers. In the present century, the blame for handicap has sometimes been transferred from the afflicted to their parents, who were seen to be the primary cause of their children's limitations. Even today, within apparently well-informed communities, handicap is sometimes regarded as a punishment for sins or inadequacies.

In the fifteenth and sixteenth centuries the mentally handicapped were the subjects of social satire. The complex figure of the traditional clown or fool may well have originated from the unconscious humour of the village idiots. Daniel Defoe, at the end of the seventeenth century, recognized that clowns and fools had something special to offer society, and attempted to instigate special provision for them in the form of 'a public foolhouse'. He stated that:

> Care should be taken of fools, as a
> tribute to God's bounty to mankind, a
> tribute to be paid to all those who
> lack His bounty (in Ryan and Thomas, 1981, p. 84).

The findings of science

The latter half of the nineteenth century saw rapid changes and innovations in education (Preen, 1976). The emergence of the science of psychology, with its emphasis on a knowledge of the mind and its relationship to human behaviour, was an important development in the investigation of mental handicap. The pioneers were doctors whose medical training brought them into close contact with handicapped children.

One such person was Dr Jean Marc Gaspard Itard who attempted to educate the 'Wild Boy of Aveyron' in 1799. 'Victor', the wild boy, was living as an animal in the Caure Woods in Southern France, when at the age of 11 or 12 he was captured by hunters and taken to Paris. His bizarre behaviour created a great deal of interest, and Itard, a young doctor and an idealist, obtained permission to work with the boy. He believed that Victor lacked 'normal experiences', which he systematically attempted to provide. In doing so, he believed that he could enable Victor to become a civilized human being. At the end of five years, the improvements (particularly in the acquisition of speech) had not been as great as he had hoped, and Itard concluded that Victor was an 'idiot' (to use the terminology of the day) and abandoned the experiment. In fact, the improvement in the boy had been phenomenal. Pritchard (1972) stresses that,

> From being a repulsive creature, Victor had become an affectionate youth, who lived like a human being, and could even read a few words. If it was possible to do so much and achieve such success with such unpromising material both mentally and environmentally, then the way to the education of the mentally handicapped lay wide open (p. 76).

The philosopher Rousseau (1712–78), although not working directly with mentally handicapped children, also made significant contributions to methods of teaching. He used scientific observation and an analysis of the patterns of psychological and physiological growth in his research. Rousseau's approach was essentially child-centred as he believed that it was important to observe the child before engaging him in the learning process within a natural and unrestricted environment. His emphasis on observation, assessment and teaching according to each child's abilities is central to the education of pupils with severe learning difficulties today.

Edward Sequin (1812–80), inspired by the work of Rousseau and Itard, developed and implemented a 'physiological method of teaching', or sensory training. His revolutionary approach required pupils to visualize, to handle, to speak in all learning situations, and, in some cases, to undergo strict physical sequencing and patterning procedures. In order to carry out his work, Sequin brought mentally handicapped children together for instruction. Segregated provision was provided, and there was a growing awareness of the need to give financial support to schools for the handicapped, particularly in the United States of America, where he had introduced his new ideas.

Maria Montessori (1870–1952), an Italian doctor, was deeply influenced by Sequin's sense-training approach. She initiated a scientific pedagogical approach to learning through activity and devised equipment to train the senses, which was also self-instructive and self-motivating. She advocated careful training, but allowed children freedom to explore and to discover for themselves. Her methods had a profound effect on the education of mentally handicapped children in Britain. Most teachers in the Junior Training Centres of the 1950s and 1960s were familiar with her didactic materials and 'sense training' was a timetabled activity in every centre. Sense training as a discrete activity lost its popularity in the 1970s, but a renewed interest in multi-sensory approaches to curriculum development for children with profound multiple learning difficulties has emerged through the work of Ouvry (1987) and Longhorn (1988).

The desire to be of service

It was some time before the effects of the findings of science substantially altered people's attitudes to the handicapped. As a result of the Industrial Revolution, the enlightened educational provision advocated by Rousseau and others was overshadowed by the dominance of 'medical' opinions which assumed that the handicapped were social rejects, incapable of work. Asylums or institutions were set up which provided, on the one hand, protection against poverty and exploitation and, on the other, permanent segregation for passive individuals who were deemed to be in need of care and protection. These institutions were run by doctors who became 'experts' in dealing with all aspects of their patients' development, including their education. A medical model of care emerged which implied that the 'patients' were ill and exempt from the obligations of work and other social responsibilities (Parsons and Fox, 1952; Fraser, 1984). As Ford *et al*. (1982) point out, this approach focuses the attention upon an individual's suffering or illness, and attempts to alleviate the symptoms and remedy the disease. Thus, the handicapped person in an institution was likely to be 'cared for' in ways which minimized meaningful experience and resulted in reduced expectations. Fraser, in discussing these reduced experiences, suggests that the handicapping conditions result in the 'patient' accepting a dependent role.

The Education Acts of 1870, 1876, and 1880 (Board of Education, 1870; 1876; 1880), which recommended compulsory education throughout England and Wales, led to an awareness that some children with acute learning difficulties were not retarded enough to be confined to institutions. Many of these children, however, tended to restrict and disrupt the work of the lower classes in schools. Special classes often had to be set up and children in these classes, although labelled 'backward', or 'feeble-minded', were educated away from their peers but remained within the education system. However, idiots and imbeciles, ('the mentally handicapped') were, in the interests of society, placed in permanent care (Cole, 1989). It was necessary to address the resulting problems and in 1908 a Royal Commission was set up to consider the care and control of the feeble-minded, which strongly recommended that the responsibility for these children should move from the Education Authorities to a new medically-dominated Board of Control. The change further strengthened medical dominance over the disabled (Tomlinson, 1982).

However, for their less-able peers, defined under the 1913 Mental Deficiency Act (Board of Health, 1913) as idiots ('persons in whose case there exists mental defectiveness of such a degree that they are unable to guard themselves against common physical dangers') and imbeciles ('persons in whose case there exists mental defectiveness which, though not amounting to idiocy, is yet so pronounced that they are incapable of managing themselves or their affairs'), life in an institution was considered right and proper. Not only did the 1913 Act recognize four categories of defective persons: idiots, imbeciles, the feeble-minded and moral defectives, but it also categorized and graded the residential institutions. Basically there were four types of care:

- State institutions: for the most dangerous people;
- Certified institutions: mental hospitals for those capable of paying fees;
- Certified houses: fee-paying institutions for the detention of certified patients;
- Approved homes: run by voluntary agencies for patients who might pay fees or receive supported placements.

Certification for these institutions was carried out by qualified medical practitioners, whom it was still thought could provide solutions to all problems. However, the dependent model of care, or 'warehouse model', provided by the institutions was causing concern (Miller and Gwynne, 1974). Consequently, in 1929 the Wood Committee (Board of Education and Board of Control, 1929) recommended that 'the defective' should render the community some service, however modest, in an effort to gain some self-respect. This Committee, whose original brief was to examine the educational provision for the category of defective person (labelled as feeble-minded in the Act) was to some extent in advance of the thinking of the day.

The 1944 Education Act (Ministry of Education, 1944) included genuine attempts to bring the education of handicapped children back into the education sector. Local Education Authorities were now required to meet the needs of backward children. The certification of idiots, imbeciles and the feeble-minded was abolished, and children considered capable of education were given the right to a place in a school. The Act was a watershed, but unfortunately, although all handicapped children became the responsibility of Local Education Authorities, a small proportion (approximately 10 per cent) were considered 'ineducable' and were excluded from education. They became the responsibility of the Local Health Authorities and some of the more able were cared for in Occupation Centres which were later renamed Junior Training Centres. Many children, however, were placed in institutions or left without adequate help at home. The medical profession still influenced the lives of 'mentally defective' children, and was responsible for making educational judgements.

The first Occupation Centres were run by philanthropists, including Elfrida Rathbone, and were voluntarily funded. By 1959, however, only 20 were being run by voluntary bodies; the remaining 415 were funded by Local Health Authorities (Pritchard, 1963; 1972). The centres, which were often housed in church halls, kept children occupied and provided some relief for parents. Staff were caring and looked after the physical needs of the children, but lacked appropriate training.

The first training courses were also opened by a voluntary organization. The National Association for Mental Health (now MIND) set up one-year full-time courses in the post-war period, which concentrated on early child development and a child-centred approach to teaching. Consequently, the quality of care offered to 'mentally defective' children began to improve dramatically. The 1959 Mental Health Act identified the need for further developments and renamed the Occupation Centres, Training Centres. Under the Act, Local Health Authorities had the power, in the case of a child of school age, to compel attendance if no adequate comparable training was being 'received' (Section 12), and also to provide residential accommodation at or near a Training Centre if necessary. These changes in legislation resulted in an extended building programme, normally based on primary school designs. Consequently, the centres, which officially catered for pupils from 5 to 16 years, but included those in their 20s, lacked specialist rooms and were equipped with infant lavatories and wash-hand basins, for infants. Many were built in areas isolated from mainstream schools, and the buildings, many of which are still in use today, have had a restrictive effect on the social integration of pupils.

Under the 1959 Act, the pupils were 'recategorized'. Those who had previously been termed idiots or imbeciles under the 1913 Mental Deficiency Act, were now called severely subnormal (SSN); the feeble-minded were termed subnormal. The definition of severe subnormality in the Act did little to acknowledge that those so labelled could ever become full and valued members of society and medical consideration influenced their training.

> Severe subnormality, a state of arrest or incomplete development of mind which includes subnormality of intelligence and is of such a nature or degree that the patient is incapable of living an independent life or of guarding himself against serious exploitation, or will be so incapable when of an age to do so (Sec.4 [2]).

This definition of severe subnormality and subnormality depended on the results of intelligence tests, the most popular of which was the Stanford Binet Intelligence Scale. Subnormals were considered to have an Intelligent Quotient of between 50 and 75; severely subnormals 50 or below. Both groups of children were believed to have low mental levels which led to the assumption that they were mentally, emotionally and socially immature. Consequently, teachers (or Assistant Supervisors as they were then called) in the Junior Training Centres adopted a nursery/infant school curriculum regardless of the age of the pupil. In fact, the word 'curriculum' was not part of the vocabulary, but the term 'training' stated in the 1959 Act summed up the methods of education used.

H. C. Gunzburg, Senior Psychologist at Monyhull Hospital, Birmingham, introduced a wider view of training. He emphasized that the aim of the Junior Training Centre was not only to make the fullest use of the abilities the pupils had, but to develop skills and knowledge through individualized training programmes. He firmly believed that, in order to be accepted by society, the severely subnormal person should be taught:

> those habits and skills which will make him socially acceptable; assisting him in learning how to live with others and how to make himself useful; and developing as much as possible his ability to use and understand spoken language, because language provides the primary link between the individual and the community (Gunzburg, 1963, p. 4).

His teaching and training programmes stressed self-help, socialization, occupation and communication and were geared to realistic goals, based on a structured approach. He developed a set of Progress Assessment Charts (PACs) which not only gave a graphic representation of the child's strengths and weaknesses in the four areas, but also allowed teachers to monitor the child's progress, or lack of it, after teaching. The Charts are still used today, and have paved the way for other innovative methods of assessment.

Public awareness of mental subnormality was raised in 1960 by World Mental Health Year and greater attention was given to those mentally and physically handicapped children who were in hospitals. They were usually the more 'difficult' children, who for many reasons could not remain in the community and were often completely separated from their families. The quality of the training and the care they received was frequently inferior and the predominantly medical approach was detrimental to the needs of the developing child. These children were often so deprived of human attention that they developed bizarre habits and repetitive behaviour (Oswin, 1978).

The 1959 Mental Health Act also emphasized the need for community care and the value of small family environments which had been highlighted by the Brooklands experiment in 1960. Sixteen children from the Fountain Hospital, a large impersonal London mental deficiency hospital, were taken to live in a country house (Brooklands) for a two-year period. Staffing ratios were high, and the children were exposed to the kinds of activities found in nursery schools. The children all had serious problems of aggression, withdrawal or high dependency on adults. They were matched with a control group at the hospital and during the experiment the Brooklands children progressed in all areas of development in comparison with the control group. The results made a major contribution to the planning of residential care (Tizard, 1962).

The need to provide better training for the staff of the Junior Training Centres and hospital schools was paramount. In 1964 a new body, The Training Council for Teachers of the Mentally Handicapped, coordinated staff training and introduced two-year training courses. A new professional began to emerge, who had a thorough knowledge of normal child development based on an understanding of the work of Piaget and Bruner. The work of Bowlby (1953) was essential reading, and led to an understanding of the need for children to experience a warm, intimate and continuous relationship with an adult as a basis for intellectual, emotional and social development.

Training programmes, based on research into the learning processes of the severely subnormal, were introduced.

A good demonstration of this progressive work was a multi-disciplinary social training programme for mentally handicapped adolescents. Called the Slough Project, it was initiated by the major training organization, the National Association for Mental Health. The Project's aims were to prepare young people for work and independence within sheltered housing in the community. Thirty young people of both sexes lived in 'villas' in family units and went to work each day. There was an emphasis on training, on relevant skills and on the development of relationships. Despite impressive results, the project closed after six and a half years (in the late-1960s) due to a lack of funding.

Another innovator in the 1960s and 1970s was Mildred Stevens, a teacher who later became the chief coordinator of one of the new training courses. She was concerned with school/parental partnerships, assessment based on the identification of needs, and creative teaching. Her three books, written in the late 1960s and the 1970s, were challenging and were based on her own teaching experiencces and her observations of her students' work. Much is still applicable. She vehemently maintained that, given stimulating teaching, children were 'educable' (Stevens, 1968; 1971; 1978).

The result of these developments was the Education (Handicapped Children) Act which transferred the responsibility for the severely subnormal from the Health Authorities to the control of the Local Education Authorities from 1971. The Junior Training Centres became special schools and the children attending them were entitled to special education (Heddell, 1980). In the same year, 1971, the White Paper *Better Services for the Mentally Handicapped* (DHSS, 1971) was published. It proposed an acceleration of the shift in emphasis from care in hospital to care in the community. It also set out:

> 3 (ii) To invite greater sympathy and tolerance on the part of the public for the mentally handicapped in their own local communities, and to stress the importance of the help they can give through voluntary services (p. 1).

The 1970s were highly significant in the development of educational services for the mentally handicapped. It was at last recognized that there are not two sorts of children, those who are handicapped and those who are not, but that all children have the basic right to education. The mentally handicapped became known as

'Educationally Subnormal' (severe or mild) and were accepted into education. The major event of the decade, however, was undoubtedly the publication of the Warnock Report (DES, 1978) which made a brave attempt to dispense with categorization and the consequent stigma. The Committee proposed a general framework which was not based on the type or degree of handicap or disability but on Special Educational Needs. It estimated that one child in five would have Special Educational Needs at some time during his school career, and therefore would require some form of special educational provision. Members of the Committee recognized three priority areas: pre-school education, further education for young people over the age of 16 and teacher training. The report recommended that all initial teacher training courses should include a special education element, and that in-service education on the teaching of children with special needs should be available to all teachers.

The report had a mixed reception. Professionals welcomed its careful, thorough and wide-ranging recommendations. Adams (1986), however, sums up the adverse criticism: the new definitions were vague and imprecise; underlying social causes of deprivation should have been dealt with; and gifted children were virtually ignored. More significantly,

> in a period of rapidly rising unemployment especially for the young and unqualified, it was wrong to assume that meaningful and satisfying 'work' would be an attainable goal for the vast majority of young people with special educational needs, who instead should have an education directed towards preparing them for long-term (often lifetime) unemployment and 'leisure' (p. 9).

The recommendations led to the 1981 Education Act which, although it did little to develop the Warnock Committee's three priority areas, emphasized a single population of children, some of whom needed additional help. This assistance had to be specifically developed for each child after individual assessment of his educational requirements, possibly resulting in the Local Education Authority making a formal statement of need. The Act also made a praise-worthy attempt to end segregation. It assumed that all children should be educated in mainstream schools, unless their needs could not be met; separate provision in special schools should be the exception rather than the rule. It is disappointing that the three priority areas were not fully accepted in the legislation, but as critics point out, this would have required extra financial resources (Adams, 1986; Freeman and Gray, 1989; Goacher et al., 1988).

Instead, the Act focused attention on those aspects of the Warnock Report which were less costly: procedures of assessment and parental involvement. In a research study on the implementation and effects of the Act, Goacher *et al.* (1988) emphasize that it attempts to bring about changes in policy, practices and attitudes despite inadequate resources. One direct result was agitation for equal rights for people with severe difficulties in learning. Better accommodation, opportunities for education and employment and freedom of choice were crucial concerns for service providers. The principles of normalization (Wolfensberger, 1972), which included the right to a normal pattern of living, were emphasized in many of the policy statements of the support services.

Although the 1988 Education Reform Act (DES, 1988) stated that all pupils are entitled to a 'broad and balanced curriculum', of which the National Curriculum forms a part, the particular needs of pupils with severe learning difficulties were not always fully considered. The consequent danger, therefore, is that history might be repeated and that the inevitable central control of the curriculum may lead to the segregation and marginalization of pupils with severe learning difficulties. Regrettably, the first documents failed to mention these pupils and, as Ware (1990) indicated,

> the view of experts in the field was that the National Curriculum was unlikely to be applied to schools for such pupils, and that it would not be appropriate for them (p. 11).

Ware does not identify 'the experts', but there were clear indications that this group of pupils had, once again, been ignored or overlooked. Fortunately, the acceptance of 'entitlement' for all children throughout the statutory schooling period from 5 to 16 years, has prompted parents and educationalists to exert pressure in order to ensure access. Nevertheless, Sections 17 to 19 of the Act do allow parts of the National Curriculum to be modified and although the Secretary of State is not expected to exempt whole categories of pupils, particular interpretations of the Act could set the clock back by 20 years (Mittler, 1990).

The documents issued by the National Curriculum Council in 1989 provided more hopeful indicators in the apparent confirmation that pupils with severe learning difficulties should be able to take part in the National Curriculum. Circular No. 5 states:

> As reported in NCC's consultation reports on the Core Subjects, the great majority of respondents strongly supported participation and

were opposed to exemption. NCC wishes to reaffirm this principle of active participation by the complete range of pupils with SEN (including those with profound and multiple learning difficulties) whether they are in special, primary, middle or secondary schools, with or without statements (NCC, 1989).

It is to be hoped, therefore, that all teachers of pupils with severe learning difficulties will continue to respond with energy and enthusiasm to the very real challenges of facilitating access. The future will at times seem bleak; the benefits will be incalculable. Fagg *et al.* (1990) are concerned with positive, active approaches:

> The National Curriculum offered a positive way forward for pupils with special educational needs to become a more integral part of the community and society. All state schools will now be sharing common terminology and curriculum. Pupils in special schools may more easily participate in educational activities with their mainstream peers, discussion between teachers now having a common framework. Breadth and balance in educational provision can therefore be increased within special and mainstream schools (p. 27).

The National Curriculum, despite the problems that it creates, must now be seen as a confirmation that all pupils, whatever their talents or difficulties, can be full and valued members of society.

References

Adams, F. (1986) *Special Education*. Essex: Longman.

Board of Education (1870) *The Elementary Education Act* (The Forster Act). London: HMSO.

Board of Education (1876) *The Elementary Education Act* (The Sandon Act). London: HMSO.

Board of Education (1880) *The Elementary Education Act* (The Mundella Act). London: HMSO.

Board of Education and Board of Control (1929) *Report of the Mental Deficiency Committee* (The Wood Report). London: HMSO.

Board of Health (1913) *Mental Deficiency Act*. London: HMSO.

Bowlby, J. (1953) *Child Care and the Growth of Love*. Harmondsworth: Penguin.

Cole, T. (1989) *Apart or A Part? Integration and the Growth of British Special Education*. Milton Keynes: Open University Press.

Department of Education and Science (1978) *Special Educational Needs: Report of the Committee of Enquiry into the Education of Handicapped Children and Young People* (The Warnock Report). London: HMSO.

Department of Education and Science (1981) *Education Acdt*. London: HMSO.

Department of Education and Science (1988) *Education Reform Act 1988*. London: HMSO.

Department of Health and Social Security (1971) *Better Services for the Mentally Handicapped*, Cmnd 7212. London: HMSO.

Fagg, S., Aherne, P., Skelton, S. and Thornber, A. (1990) *Entitlement for All in Practice*. London: David Fulton.

Ford, J., Mongdon, D. and Whelan, M. (1982) *Special Education and Social Control: Invisible Disasters*. London: Routledge and Kegan Paul.

Fraser, B. (1980) 'The meaning of handicap in children', *Child Care: Health and Development*, 6, pp. 83–91.

Fraser, B. (1984) *Society, Schools and Handicap*. Stratford upon Avon: NCSE.

Freeman, A. and Gray, H. (1989) *Organising Special Educational Needs: A Critical Approach*. London: Croom Helm.

Goacher, B., Evans, J., Welton, J. and Wedell, K. (1988) *Policy and Provision for Special Educational Needs. Implementing the 1981 Education Act*. London: Cassell.

Gunzburg, H. C. (1963) *Junior Training Centres*. London: National Association for Mental Health.

Heddell, F. (1980) *Accident of Birth*. London: British Broadcasting Corporation.

Hewett, M. and Forness, S. R. (1974) *Education of Exceptional Learners*. Boston: Allyn & Bacon.

Longhorn, F. (1988) *A Sensory Curriculum for Very Special People*. London: Souvenir Press.

Miller, E. J. and Gwynne, G. R. (1974) *A Life Apart: A Pilot Study of Residential Institutions for the Physically Handicapped and the Young Chronically Sick*. London: Tavistock Publications.

Ministry of Education (1944) *Education Act 1944*. London: HMSO.

Mittler, P. (1990) 'Foreword: From entitlement to access' in Fagg, S. Aherne P., Skelton, S. and Thornber, A. (Eds) *Entitlement for All in Practice*. London: David Fulton.

National Curriculum Council (1989) *Circular No. 5: Implementing the National Curriculum – Participation by Pupils with Special Educational Needs*. York: NCC.

Oswin, M. (1978) *Children Living in Long-stay Hospitals*. Suffolk: Havenham Press.

Ouvry, C. (1987) *Educating Children with Profound Handicaps*. Kidderminster: BIMH.

Parsons, T. and Fox, R. (1952) 'Illness, therapy and the modern American family', *Journal of Social Issues*, 8, 4, pp. 31–44.

Preen, B. (1976) *Schooling for the Mentally Retarded*. Queensland: University of Queensland Press.

Pritchard, D. (1963) *Education and the Handicapped 1760–1960*. London: Routledge and Kegan Paul.

Pritchard, D. (1972) 'The development of educational provision for mentally handicapped children', in Laing, A. (Ed.) *Educating Mentally Handicapped Children*. Swansea: University College of Swansea.

18

Roberts, N. (1960) *Everybody's Business. The 1959 Mental Health Act and the Community*. London: National Association for Mental Health.

Ryan, J. and Thomas, P. (1981) 'Mental handicap: the historical background', in Swann, W. (Ed.) *The Practice of Special Education*. Milton Keynes: Open University Press.

Stevens, M. (1968) *Observing Children who are Severely Subnormal*. London: Edward Arnold.

Stevens, M. (1971) *The Educational Needs of Severely Subnormal Children*. London: Edward Arnold.

Stevens, M., (1978) *Observe then Teach* (2nd edn). London: Edward Arnold.

Tizard, J. (1962) 'The residential care of mentally handicapped children', in Richards, R.W. (Ed.) *Proceedings of the Scientific Study of Mental Deficiency, 1960*. Dagenham: May & Baker.

Tomlinson, S. (1982) *A Sociology of Special Education*. London: Routledge and Kegan Paul.

Tredgold, R.F. and Soddy, K. (1956) *Tredgold's Textbook of Mental Deficiency* (9th edn). London: Bailliere, Tindall & Cox.

Ware, J. (1990) 'The National Curriculum for pupils with severe learning difficulties', in Daniels, H. and Ware, J. (Eds) *Special Educational Needs and the National Curriculum*. London: Kogan Page.

Wolfensberger, W. (1972) *The Principle of Normalisation in Human Services*. Toronto: National Institute on Mental Retardation.

Wood, S. and Shears, B. (1986) *Teaching Children with Severe Learning Difficulties. A Radical Re-appraisal*. London: Croom Helm.

CHAPTER 2

Parents' Views

Joginder Phull, Frances Young and Betty Cowley

Introduction

It is important for professionals to recognize that parents are the primary advocates for members of a family who need to address problems resulting from the presence of a child with severe learning difficulties. In addition, they are not only the 'first educators' of their children (DES, 1989; Mittler and Mittler, 1982) but they will also have acquired the expertise to make essential information about their children available to all members of the 'professional educational team'.

Opportunities for the establishment of parents as partners in their children's education are fully explored in Chapter 8. It should also be borne in mind that the National Curriculum is designed to foster active parental involvement in the support of teaching programmes and assessment in addition to the encouragement offered by the Education Reform Act (ERA) for parents to participate as governors of their children's schools. It is becoming self-evident that a climate which promotes and encourages full interaction will enable the parents (of past and present children) to contribute to the development of curriculum policies which will equip all children to take their place in society.

The different perspectives of the three contributors to this chapter have been determined by their contacts with professionals, by society's expectations and by their perceptions of what the education system, in

19

the widest sense, had to offer their children. Each of them has made a distinctive and active contribution to his or her child's school. We, as professionals, must learn from them.

Kiran's first twenty years. *Joginder Phull*

We, like most parents, were excited and looked forward to the arrival of a new baby, our second. I went to see my wife, Gurmeet, at the hospital as soon as I learnt of our daughter's birth, accompanied by my 5-year-old son, Sukhvinder. The ward sister greeted us with a wonderful smile, took us to my wife's bedside and told us that both mother and baby were doing well. My wife was still sedated but very happy and showed us the tiny bundle of joy lying in the adjacent cot. She looked gorgeous. The sister straightened the cot blanket, pointed to the baby's full head of natural black hair and remarked, 'How lovely. She is cute, just like a pretty doll'.

A week later, on the day that the baby was due to come home, she found difficulty in swallowing her feed. A doctor who examined her suggested that she should stay in hospital for a few more days. He did, however, allow my wife to go home and made arrangements for her to visit the hospital at any time to feed, wash and hold the baby. In a few days she made good progress and was able to take her feeds without the need of a tube. We were naturally very pleased when the doctor, after he had finished his morning round, told us that we could take her home the following day.

The consultant paediatrician who had examined her asked to see us. Gurmeet and I arrived in his office and were joined by another doctor and the matron. It still did not dawn on me that anything was seriously wrong until the consultant dropped a bombshell:

> I am afraid your baby is mentally handicapped and has what is known in the medical field as Down's syndrome. She may be seriously retarded, she may not be able to walk, talk, or feed herself. She certainly will not look like other children. I am sorry but there is nothing I or anyone else can do to help. Sub-normal babies are sometimes rejected by their parents and institutionalized. If you wish to put the baby in a home, talk to the matron here and she will put you in touch with the right authorities. Are there any questions you would like to ask?

What could we ask? We were stunned and shocked with feelings akin to those of the bereaved. The consultant could not have been more direct or to the point. His realistic approach was probably appropriate as it can be as shattering and frustrating not to be told, as it is to find out gradually. On reflection, however, what hurt us most was that the experts, who must have known what we were going through, were of little or no help at all in providing reassurance, support services or practical guidance. We decided straight away to take our baby home and to love her for what she was. We named her Kiran, which in our language, means a ray – a ray of hope. While there is hope there is a future and the future leads to progress!

My wife has a resolute and steadfast faith in the Sikh religion and firmly believes that we are all God's creatures, great or small, normal or otherwise – God's will prevails. Sikhism is not only a modern religion but is a practical way of life and in its scriptures, the Adi Granth, the most potent theme is that all life is a great divine drama and that we are all actors in the dramatic play of God. His creation is the stage where each of us is destined to play a specific part and is required to perform to our full capacity. How well or badly we play or enjoy the part depends mainly upon our determination, commitment, ability, insight and understanding, as well as on the way in which we relate to the whole drama.

This religious philosophy, when accepted within the context of a handicapped child or a major mishap, simply implies that while accepting God's will, one makes allowances for personal endeavour and faith. Everything does not depend upon Karma alone. It leaves no room for the apportioning of blame. It advocates mutual support, positive attitudes and a constructive approach to otherwise desperate situations. Our religious belief helped us to accept our child's handicap. We have always been aware of her limitations and have made the necessary adjustments but have not let the problems overwhelm our whole existence.

Kiran came home to a large household as, at that time, we lived with my in-laws in an extended family unit. Uncles, aunts, nephews and nieces were all willing to share their affection and to give their time in caring for Kiran. The advantages of an extended family far outweigh the disadvantages in bringing up a handicapped child.

What is lost in the way of privacy and independence is amply compensated for by the constant support available. The love, care and help offered by the family could be seen as an intrusion; we think not, although this picture of a 'full house' may suggest to some 'experts' that under such living conditions mother and child may not easily form that special bond so vital for a child's development. An undoubted benefit is that an extended family system provides parents with a wide range of opportunities to learn about bringing up children under the supervision of older and more experienced relatives. At first, Kiran demanded her mother's undivided attention at feed times and if one of us took over she would start crying and would refuse the bottle. Later she quietly accepted the feed from any of us.

We all soon learnt to handle, to love and to communicate with Kiran. The male members of our family too were always ready to play the mothering role, unusual in Asian families, when necessary. Kiran made slow and steady progress throughout her infancy and started to take solids when she was 3 months old. Sometimes we were given conflicting advice by the family doctor, child clinic or friends but each time we followed our intuition and common sense. She was about a year old before she could hold her head upright and develop control. We were overjoyed when at the age of 18 months she started to walk, for the doctors had said that she would not reach this stage of her development until she was between 3 and 5. Gurmeet had managed to toilet-train Kiran by the time she was 3.

Kiran had been very lucky to have been brought up in a pleasant and comfortable environment with plenty of people around her. She has always been treated as a full member of the family and we have always tried to get her accepted within the wider community, although at first we found it difficult to get used to the stares and tactless remarks, particularly in new surroundings, which increased in frequency as Kiran grew older.

A year later we moved into our own house and found Kiran a place in a well-equipped council nursery for 'normal' children in the vicinity. She soon settled in and learnt to mix and play with children of her own age. The staff loved her and she loved going to the nursery. The only thing that limited her interactions with other people was her inability to communicate fully. Her speech was slurred, limited to single sentences and, at times, unintelligible owing to her large tongue. We found it difficult, but by the time she was of school age she was beginning to understand English and Punjabi (her mother tongue) although her speech was still very restricted.

We were given a choice of two special schools. Gurmeet and I visited both and selected the one which we thought most suitable. For the first few days Gurmeet decided to stay with Kiran in her classroom in order to get her used to her new environment. The staff were impressed with the way in wich my wife responded, not only to Kiran's but also other children's needs. A week later the headteacher telephoned and offered her a job in the school and she has been working there ever since. Kiran had little difficulty in settling down as she was lucky enough to have a familiar face in the classroom. Later, in Kiran's own interest, Gurmeet asked for a transfer to the upper school as we both wanted her to learn to become independent.

Kiran has always managed to establish a special relationship with her teachers and other members of staff and we have taken an active part in her education. We started a 'diary system' with her nursery class teacher and continued this invaluable link. It enabled us to inform the teachers of any interesting incidents or visits, functions or other happenings at home in which Kiran was involved. The teachers in turn kept us in touch not only with Kiran's progress and any problems that she encountered in the classroom, but also with general events in the school. We were consequently able to reinforce Kiran's school work, to learn about her friends, her likes and dislikes in the class and, most important to us, her achievements as perceived by professionals.

Over the years we have found that most teachers are keen to cooperate fully with us, although some were initially hostile to the idea of a diary system. We were invited to all school social functions and parents evenings, not only through the normal official invitations but by personal invitations to visit the school through the 'diary'. In short, we became involved in school fund-raising activities and were founder members of the Parents' Support Group started by the headteacher in conjunction with a consultant paediatrician at a large city hospital.

The primary aim of the group was to bring together parents of children with similar disabilities in order to help each other through the exchange of ideas and information. The group was unique in that the coordinator arranges for selected members to visit the parents of newly diagnosed children to offer practical advice and help. The first time Gurmeet and I visited such a family, I admit we were apprehensive, not knowing whether or not the door would be slammed in our faces, but we need not have worried. We were received courteously and a personal and friendly relationship developed. The parents, who were worried and wondered what the next few years would bring, were reassured to see us with Kiran, who behaved well and of whom we spoke highly, with love and pride. These parents soon joined the goup meetings and enjoyed the benefits of other parents' experiences of bringing up handicapped children. This gave us a feeling of purpose.

As time passed Kiran graduated to higher classes and then to the upper school. We were, at times, over-protective and as a result she became rather quiet and reserved and showed little initiative and assertiveness. The school, however, helped her to be more outgoing, gave her confidence and encouraged her to take initiatives. Later, she developed the confidence to recite the opening prayers at charity functions organized at local Sikh temples and raised hundreds of pounds for the school fund. She learnt many skills and became more competent at dressing, undressing, washing and bathing herself and also helped with the household chores.

Kiran stayed at school beyond the age of 16 as it was thought that she would benefit from an extended period of education. In her case emphasis was placed on the development of the skills needed to meet the demands of adult life. At the age of 19 she left school and we started to look for possible post-19 provisions. We were utterly dismayed not only by the apparent lack of choice of training places accessible to young people with learning difficulties but also by the shortage of information available to parents. The result was a petition to the city council, meetings with councillors and letters from the parents of handicapped children to their MPs urging them to provide better resources for the adult training of young handicapped school leavers. Although the present provision includes Adult Training Centres (run by Social Services) and courses at the Local Education Authorities' colleges of further education for post-19 handicapped youngsters, there is a lack of an adequate and comprehensive service of day-care and training.

Kiran was selected for a place on a two-year course at a local college and we found the staff to be a very helpful and conscientious team of dedicated professionals. A weekly programme was published and displayed, which enabled both the students and parents to be involved and to contribute to the learning process. As a parent representative on the steering committee of the course, I appreciated how much hard work and planning had been done. Kiran benefited tremendously and amazed us with her capacity to learn so much in just two years. Her progress could have been due to the teaching methods or perhaps as a late developer she was at her most receptive. She also gained in confidence and left college at the end of the course for training at an Employment Preparation Unit where she has now spent just over a year. We were pleased when she was recently assessed and selected as a suitable candidate for training in engineering assembly and she is now enjoying her work in the engineering section of the Unit. Hopefully she will find herself a job which she will also enjoy and will eventually be able to live in the community.

Over the past 20 years with the grace of God, the support and encouragement of our family and friends, and the help of the professionals, our hopes and dreams for Kiran have to a great extent been realized.

Arthur's education. *Frances Young*

The fundamental problem for parents of the very severely handicapped is the need to come to terms with their children's acute limitations. One always hopes and imagines that things will get better and services for the mentally handicapped and their families tend to stress the possibility of positive progress and success. This may be an excellent reaction against past practice, but for families with a child as profoundly handicapped as Arthur, it can create more pressures, both practical and emotional, than it is possible to cope with. It increases the sense of failure, and creates feelings of guilt and inadequacy, for both parents and teachers.

Arthur was a full-term baby but of premature weight. As naïve, first-time parents we had no suspicion that things were wrong, although experienced medical workers must have known that pre-natal development had been retarded. When 8 months old he was diagnosed as microcephalic; some six months later his 'education' began. We moved to a new locality and our new general practitioner put us in contact with the Inspector for Special Education who introduced us to the Doman-Delacato method. Our lives became dominated by the need to stimulate Arthur, and to undertake 'patterning' with him twice a day. We were desperate to try anything to increase his potential and, as he was an only child, we still had hope!

At a remarkably early age (given what we now know about his disability) Arthur learned to crawl. We had been led to believe that mobility would increase his learning capacity and we were delighted that he enjoyed movement and that he was able to race around on all fours. Sadly, he did so only for the sensation for he remained profoundly unresponsive and, if we are honest, there was little eye contact. We had begun to delude ourselves that he was beginning to respond. He was, however, extremely limited in his play and restricted himself to rattles with which he developed a very complex set of hand movements. He never succeeded with other objects, despite all our efforts to prompt and interest him. He was incapable of sitting up unaided, and despite his crawling ability, he was unable to fetch a favourite toy seen at the other side of the room. He lacked the instinct to place objects in his mouth, and feeding remained a persistent problem.

His ability to crawl developed his potential in a single area and masked the seriousness of his disability. It fed hope but ultimately made the disillusion and the physical problems more difficult to bear. The 'side-effects' were not apparent until much later. In his teens he suffered weeks of discomfort with his legs in plaster, stretching contracted tendons, and for a while a complete loss of independent mobility. Further physical consequences of his tendency to settle on the floor in a particular position and stay there for hours still create problems. We remain in a 'Catch-22' situation. Although I have for years blamed myself for letting him sit on his legs in a kneeling position, it was an almost inevitable consequence of having encouraged him to crawl early. He did at least crawl around looking for his favourite toys, but his dawning initiative came too late. He has not sufficiently developed his muscles to be able to take advantage of his 'progress' – in fact, his body became so twisted that his 'walking' (with assistance) regressed, and now his hips are dislocated and any attempts to walk are a thing of the past. He reached the peak of his achievement when he left school.

Baby number two arrived, and we began to realize that our lives could not be dominated by the supposed needs of a handicapped child. It took us some time to develop a balanced view, but the newcomer was unusually bright and, as soon as he could crawl, was 'into everything' including Arthur's exercises! Withdrawal of attention would clearly create deep jealousies, and compromises had to be made. I am now convinced that the ability to adjust indicates maturity in the parents of handicapped children; the desire to 'do something' can easily become obsessive and deeply unhealthy. Programmes like Doman-Delacato exploit the natural reactions of desperate parents, and create psychological blockages which make balanced attitudes in family life difficult to achieve.

Pre-school experiences for Arthur included time in a day-nursery, where it was hoped that interaction with 'normal' children would provide valuable additional stimulation. Looking back I am sceptical about how much he really gained. I suspect he became more nervous of other people; when toddlers barged into him, he was defenceless. We also made mistakes in attempting to define Arthur's relationship with his younger brother as, with hindsight, it would have been advisable to have put both boys into the same nursery group. We should have realized that the younger boy would probably have protected Arthur and not been jealous of him, as we had feared. Another valuable opportunity missed! However, that it now water under the bridge and we have to accept that it is easy to be wise after the event.

Arthur was admitted to a special school at the age of 5 which was unusual at the time. He remained in the same class for several years and in the same school until he left at the age of 18. Teachers continued to struggle with the same self-help skills throughout his school life: feeding and toiletting. The reality is that at 24 he is still in nappies and still has to be fed. It could be said that he has made no progress over those years, but in fact Arthur developed in many small ways. Since leaving school he has become noticeably more responsive and curious about the things around him. He now gets bored by long periods at home and enjoys going out. Previously, he was happier to be left alone in peace and appeared insecure in unfamiliar environments. This gradual development in his responsiveness has been helped by our insistence that he should go out and sometimes get away from home for short periods in order to learn to adapt to new and different environments. We persisted despite his occasional adverse reactions. He may have gained from these experiences, but it is difficult to identify the exact benefits of much of his education, particularly in terms of notable achievements.

This may appear hypercritical and create the impression that as parents we are dissatisfied with the education that Arthur received. Such an idea is far from the truth as we have always believed that the school responded sensitively to our son and was remarkably flexible in coping with his most difficult behaviours. Nevertheless, teachers as well as parents must address the reality of handicap and both need to 'cope' with failure. The ideology of our society is success-orientated, and as 'success' tends to be defined in terms of units of progress to-wards normality, the reality of 'non-progress' is far too demoralizing to admit. There are times, however, when it cannot be avoided. I remember the day the school doctor told me of how she had had to help the staff to realize that when Arthur had a fit and stopped breath-ing, nothing could be done and that he might die. I was just grateful for her pragmatic approach and perhaps it should be more common.

Theory is easy; practice is more difficult. It must be appreciated that parents and teachers may be at different 'emotional' stages in their capacity to cope with handicap and that if help in coming to terms with the reality of failure is offered at the wrong moment, profound hurt may be caused. On one occasion I found it difficult to accept the advice of a specialist that I should not let my normal child suffer for the sake of my handicapped son; later I appreciated his wisdom.There are times when pressure for progress and collaboration between school and home on specific goals can be more than a family can take. It is therefore vital that all involved in the education of the profoundly handicapped should be sensitive to what is and what is not possible.

The most difficult period in our family life was during the babyhood of our third child. His arrival meant that we had again to cope with two babies; one of them large and extremely difficult. For Arthur these were distressing times and he rejected all physical contact: dressing, bathing, changing nappies, eating – even loving! In many areas his slow progress stopped and he regressed. Unfortunately, Arthur could not tell us what was wrong and I responded with all the desperate emotions of a young mother to a baby who cries continuously. No one could help. Doctors prescribed sedatives, to no effect. By now we had lost all hope; survival was all we could ask for.

And yet some professionals continued to talk about progress and development and advised us on ways of encouraging Arthur to feed himself. It was utterly inappropriate. I could not cope and was left feeling guilty and inadequate. During this difficult and apparently interminable period, Arthur's miserable existence seemed pointless and progress appeared beyond his grasp. Hindsight helps! Arthur has always reacted to discomfort and we now realize that he was cutting his second teeth. We have recently endured a similar period; we think it is wisdom teeth! It is still hard to take, but we now believe that a different Arthur will soon re-emerge.

On reflection, I am convinced that 'progress' and 'pressure for progress' can actually inhibit the development of valuable qualities. Trust and respect, and relaxed and accepting relationships in which love can flourish, are precious attributes. Unfortunately, however, in some circumstances love for a handicapped child can become possessive and dictatorial. The consequent damage can be as great as the withdrawal of all stimulation.

Even after mature reflection, it is still difficult to decide whether things could have been different. I now believe that much of Arthur's progress was 'inbuilt', and that many of our efforts to force it have created additional problems for him and for us. He learned to resist our help and to be utterly uncooperative, he became distrustful of people and my anxiety as a mother exaggerated his reactions. Life has improved since I learnt to relax, to accept the reality of his handicap, to stop blaming myself for making things worse by my own mistakes, to enjoy him for what he is, and to have enough respect for him to leave him alone when he does not want my attention.

Note

This section is an adaptation of Young, F. (1990) *Face to Face: A Narrative Eassay in the Theology of Suffering*, pp. 196–202. *Edinburgh: T. T. Clark*.

Gaynor's adolescence *Betty Cowley*

I was told, two weeks after she was born, that my eldest daughter was mentally handicapped. I found it difficult to plan for the future and could only cope by taking one day at a time. At first I never worried about her sexuality. I believed that she was too profoundly handicapped to become sexually aware and, in all honesty, I was relieved that I would never have to acknowledge her 'growing up'.

My daughter menstruated at 13 and quickly developed physically but it came as quite a shock to realize that my 'baby' was becoming an attractive young woman. I now realize that most parents of young mentally handicapped people over-protect them at this vulnerable age and continue to treat them as children. My younger teenage children are now 'feeling their feet', demanding more freedom and even making mistakes, but Gaynor is 'protected' and shielded.

We were shocked when Gaynor showed signs of sexual awareness. At first I noticed when I got her up in the morning that she had placed objects between her legs: talc bottles, teddies, etc. She started masturbating and clearly found the activities pleasurable. My initial reaction was to stop her and it took much soul-searching to come to terms with the fact that she had rights over her own body. I tried at this point to find help to enable me to cope with the situation. I wrote to SPOD – the Association to Aid Sexual and Personal Relationships of People with a Disability – and they sent me leaflets and a book list. I tried to approach other parents but a typical reaction was 'Oh my child has never done anything like that!' and I began to wonder if Gaynor was an 'oddity'. I am now convinced that she is not but that many parents are unwilling to address their child's sexuality and pretend that it does not exist. My main concern is for young people at the lower-ability range, with normal physical development, but who cannot be counselled and are not able to understand how their bodies work or the feelings that they may have. I believe that in the past society avoided the issues and kept these young people 'safe', either in institutions or isolated in their own homes. I am certain that my own daughter's aggressive behaviour has at times been due to frustration.

Society is only now recognizing their needs. Some families cope at home; other young handicapped adults live in hostels and have opportunities to form relationships. Controls and careful supervision can be exercised, but is that acceptable? My daughter formed a friendship with a boy in her class when she was 16 and we were pleased because, until then, she had been a 'loner'. The boy was considerably more capable and enjoyed the role of protector but Gaynor furthered the physical side in small ways. We had good contacts with the school and, with our encouragement, the friendship developed. The boy came to tea and it was amusing to see Gaynor ignoring him completely in our presence. Unfortunately, he had a number of problems and had to move from the school. They no longer see each other but nevertheless we have had to face the fact that the relationship might have developed and we would have needed to relinquish our control to a considerable degree. We never left them alone in a room together, and, although we delude ourselves that the situation was not planned, we wonder whether or not our children will accept such restrictions on their privacy when they are 18.

Gaynor might only ever want a 'kiss and cuddle' relationship but should we deny her that chance? I know I enjoy sleeping next to someone and having the comfort of their presence, but most mentally handicapped people are denied even this simple pleasure and live a life not only of celibacy but of loneliness. Many of the handicapped are a 'new phenomenon' as medical developments over the last 30 years have ensured the survival of those who would have previously died young. Many reach adulthood with healthy bodies and natural instincts. There are now people living in the community for whom we have no role models and society has to take responsibility for the consequences of their relationships.

Concerned about Gaynor's future, we visited our GP who immediately offered the oral contraceptive, but after consideration we decided that a pill, which would have to be administered by someone other than Gaynor for 30 or more years, was not appropriate. We were then referred to the local hospital for the mentally handicapped where we were advised to consider either an inter-uterine device or Depra-Provine injections. As both methods are invasive with possible side effects and as Gaynor was unlikely to be cooperative, these options were ruled out.

At this point, it was suggested that Gaynor should be 'allowed' to have a baby, a proposal that seemed ridiculous, but as we felt that every possibility had to be carefully considered, we did not reject the idea immediately. We had been advised that pregnancy was medically inadvisable as Gaynor's small size put her at risk and that abortion might be essential. We then considered the consequences of a full-term pregnancy. Gaynor is clearly incapable of caring for a child and before adoption the fact that the mother, and possibly the father, were mentally handicapped would have to be addressed. In addition, without some form of birth control, a series of pregnancies would be a possibility.

The last option was sterilization. At first we found it repugnant, but after much thought and research we realized that it could in fact be the safest form of contraception with the least serious side effects. Her views, however, would need to be taken into account.

A satisfactory method of avoiding pregnancies does not eliminate the sexual development of the mentally handicapped and consequent problems. They will continue to need support and help to understand their bodies but I believe that the removal of the fear of pregnancy, in the case of girls, will lead to the development of positive relationships.

I would be happy to see Gaynor in a loving relationship, knowing that she was safeguarded from the risk of pregnancy. Over-protection can be stifling and will inhibit development, but I believe that parents must take their responsibilities seriously and should provide sympathetic guidance and care. I attended a funeral recently of a mentally handicapped man in his late-40s. His mother's comment at the funeral was that she was glad that he had gone before her, as she would not have the worry of leaving him 'at the mercy of society'. This statement must surely be an indictment of our society when a parent would prefer her child to die rather than be left without her own guidance. I believe that many parents have similar attitudes to their children's sexuality when they say they are 'glad' that they don't have to bother with 'that sort of thing'. Surely a caring society ought to be able to cope with the need for the mentally handicapped to form relationships and to help others to lead more independent lives.

References

Department of Education and Science (1989) *Our Changing Schools*. London: HMSO.
Mittler, P. and Mittler, H. (1982) *Partnership with Parents*. Stratford: NCSE.

CHAPTER 3

Pupils' Views

Christina Tilstone

People with learning difficulties have become increasingly critical of the ways in which professionals (including teachers) underestimate their abilities and undervalue their views. Through the self-advocacy movement people with a range of disabilities are demanding the opportunities to make decisions and exercise choices about their own lives (John, 1986; Oliver, 1989; Barton, 1989).

The first self-advocates with disabilities to make an impression on society were those with good social and communication skills. Most had physical disabilities and argued that their rights should be taken into account. They articulated their distaste for dependency-creating relationships with which professionals often enclosed them. However, in the late 1970s people with learning difficulties also made similar challenges and began to organize themselves into groups to talk about their experiences and to make joint decisions. The closure of large residential hospitals encouraged people with more severe learning difficulties either to join existing groups or to form their own. As a result of the work of Williams and Shoultz (1982), Cooper and Hersov (1986) and Clare (1990) young people have challenged the providers of services to help to create opportunities for acceptable lifestyles and relationships. An international organization 'People First' has been established and people with severe learning difficulties are now running their own International Conventions. As the self-advocacy movement has grown in strength, a variety of definitions of the term have emerged. Clare (1990), however, suggests that most definitions include or imply four basic principles which allow an individual to:

(1) Express his thoughts and feelings.
(2) Make choices and decisions.
(3) Be given information on his rights.
(4) Be allowed to make changes in his own lifestyle.

The FEU's publication, *Developing Self Advocacy Skills* (1990) claims that the starting point of self-advocacy is the

> belief that all human beings have equal value and are deserving of respect. Without this foundation of an affirmative attitude, professionals will, consciously or not, continue to give negative messages to people with disabilities about their own value and competence (p. 15).

People with severe difficulties in learning certainly believe that the label 'mental handicap' conveys negative messages about their abilities and pressure from self-advocacy groups has persuaded many organizations to eliminate these stigmatizing labels from their titles. The problem of 'labelling' is frequently raised in discussions by people with learning difficulties within the self-advocacy movement. Often pupils in schools have similar concerns and discuss the issues whether in personal and social education programmes or in informal discussions. The following exchange took place between two 14-year-olds with the teacher present.

> *Simon*:   I'm mentally handicapped.
> *Teacher*: Why?
> *Simon*:   Because my sister says so!
> *Rosie*:   I was (mentally) handicapped but I've had my teeth done. People talk to me now.
> *Teacher*: Didn't they talk to you before?
> *Rosie*:   No, they knew I was handicapped then. Now they talk to me properly.
> *Teacher*: What do you mean properly?
> *Rosie*:   Yes, you know! About dogs and cats. And things like I like.
> *Robert*:   I want my teeth done!

One possible interpretation of this discourse is that the pupils believed the solution to their problem was to be found in medically-orientated intervention. Rosie equated her handicap with her dental problems which she believed limited her opportunities for social interaction. When, in her terms, she was 'cured', her social contacts increased.

She may also have signalled that in the past people had taken little notice of her interests and it is, therefore, vitally important for teachers to listen to, and respect, their pupils' views. Only then can the information received be used to access the curriculum. Listening to pupils who have communication difficulties, or whose focus of interest is considered to be inappropriate to their chronological age, is difficult. Teachers have a natural desire to instruct and channel (and in some cases dominate) pupils' responses.

Self-advocacy is not only concerned with adult status or the transition between adolescence and adult life. The skills needed to gain control over their own lives are the ones which underpin the curriculum for all pupils of all ages. Self-awareness, decision-making, choosing and taking on responsibilities are essential competencies which allow pupils to become active participants in society and 'capable of achieving as much independence as possible' (DES, 1978, p. 5).

The National Curriculum cross-curricular elements identify a set of core skills which prepare pupils for active participation in adult society: 'All these skills are transferable, chiefly independent of content and can be developed in different contexts across the whole curriculum' (NCC, 1990, p. 3). They include communication, study skills and problem-solving. Communication has always been a high priority in the teaching of pupils with severe learning difficulties and there is evidence in the unpublished curriculum documents of many special schools that study skills have been taught directly. The published curriculum of Rectory Paddock (Staff of Rectory Paddock School, 1983) clearly reflects this trend. Teachers may, however, need to give careful consideration to the specific skills required by their pupils if they are to become independent learners. In addition, a learning environment must be provided to encourage the acquisition and practice of these skills. Chapter 7, Managing the Classroom Environment, addresses these issues.

Fowler (1990) suggests that self-reliance, self-discipline, social responsibility and the ability to work cooperatively are important study skills. The basic skills of attending, completing tasks and joint goal-setting need to be fostered and encouraged as they will help all pupils to 'learn how to learn'; 'learning how to learn' also requires pupils to use relationships as a means of bringing new opportunities to learning. Firth and Rapley (1990) identify these opportunities as 'learning about others, learning from others, learning through others and learning about ourselves'.

John and Michael were close friends, both of whom had profound learning difficulties, were non-ambulant and communicated through eye-pointing. Michael had limited mobility in his arms and hands, but was able to actuate a switch pad if placed in the correct position. John on the other hand had greater mobility and could operate the joy-stick of his wheelchair and stretch out for objects. He did, however, have a severe hearing loss. The friends had learned to cooperate on tasks and to support each other in learning activities.

In one observed cookery session, Michael used his limited movement to actuate a pressure pad linked to a symbol communication board to indicate (for John) the basic ingredients and utensils required. John manipulated his wheelchair position from which he could transfer ingredients and utensils to the designated work area. Although adult intervention was then required to finish the tasks, both used their own abilities to learn through each other.

The importance of the teacher developing the in-depth skills of observation cannot be over-emphasised, for only then will she be able to see the signals given out by some of her pupils indicating their ability to interact and cooperate. The appropriate cooperative skills can then be encouraged as steps to independent learning. Helping children with severe learning difficulties to make choices is an essential part of any teaching programme and should be encouraged from a pupil's first day at school. Making choices can be a simple activity where it is only necessary to indicate a yes/no preference, or a very complex process which may be determined by collecting information and an awareness of probable consequences.

The following list of choices about what to eat or drink is adapted from Cooper and Hersov (1986) and shows a hierarchical structure.

(1)	Whether or not to have a cup of tea.	A simple yes/no.
(2)	Tea or coffee?	A choice between two known items.
(3)	Cornflakes, Rice Krispies, Wheat Flakes or Muesli for breakfast?	A choice between a larger, but finite list of items
(4)	Which items from a given menu are to be ordered; someone else to pay.	A more complex choice of two or three related items from a larger finite list of items, plus some consideration of the other person.
(5)	Select a restaurant for a meal.	Find out the range in order to make a choice based on price, location and preference.
(6)	Describe your favourite meal in your favourite restaurant.	A choice of an almost infinite number of possible answers.

Encouraging pupils to make decisions for themselves can lead to the challenging of the learning opportunities chosen by the teacher (with her implicit values and standards) as the pupils may be in a position to make unexpected, or even unwelcomed, choices. A pupil who suddenly refuses to go horse-riding and wishes to be included in another activity which has been carefully planned for a specified number of participants, could create difficulties when 'immediate flexibility' is not possible. If pupils are to be encouraged to make choices, it is important for the school to be responsive to more sophisticated demands. It is also essential to listen constantly to the views of pupils in order to ascertain their changing curriculum needs.

A conversation with Julie, a 16-year-old, during a group discussion, alerted the teacher to the need for more individual counselling on personal and social education. Julie uses a combination of speech and a sophisticated signing system which she has devised with Makaton as a basis. Every effort has been made to record all her signals as accurately as possible.

> *Teacher*: Do you like making choices, Julie?
> *Julie*: Yes, I like choosing what I want to do.
> *Teacher*: What do you like doing?
> *Julie*: Tasks . . . . Being with Winston. Cooking. Tapes (music).
> *Teacher*: What don't you like?
> *Julie*: Assembly . . . . Going to the Sports Centre. Not eating (Julie is overweight and is on a diet).
> *Teacher*: Is is easy to make choices?
> *Julie*: Yes . . . . No . . . . Sometimes.
> *Teacher*: When is it difficult?
> *Julie*: My mum and Mrs R- (another teacher) won't let me be with Winston.
> *Teacher*: Do you know why?
> *Julie*: Babies!!

Clearly Julie was experiencing the conflicing influences that making choices involves. The decision to be put on a diet had been made for her, but was one that she was prepared to accept. The constraints on meeting Winston, however, she found unacceptable.

The decisions made for her about Winston can not be questioned here, but the dialogue emphasizes the need for teachers to listen to their pupils and respect their views. They can voice their needs but only if teachers will make time to listen. The outcome of the conversation with Julie was that the teacher was able to explore in depth with her, her sexual and relationship needs. Thus pupil and teacher moved towards a situation in which factual information on sexuality and attitudes towards her relationship with Winston could be shared. This sharing led to decision-making and action plans which brought about positive change and development. The notion of joint decision-making between pupil and teacher is central to the development of Records of Achievement (ROAs). Broadfoot (1988) emphasises that ROAs encourage more pupil-centred curriculum development, improved relationships between pupils and teachers, and active student participation in learning. Student participation in ROAs can take many forms but it usually consists of the self-evaluation of endeavour and experience and the self-appraisal of personal qualities (which may involve joint target-setting) (Russell, 1991). Records of Achievement require a teacher to change her role: from judge to witness; from provider of information to provider of opportunity; from director to partner; from authority figure to consultant; from instructor to counsellor. Only then are opportunities for active participation and the sharing of ideas maximized (Marsden, 1991).

The following transcript is part of a lengthy discussion on Records of Achievement and negotiated learning with 16- to 19-year-olds in a school for pupils with severe learning difficulties. Seventeen students from the further education unit of a school for pupils with severe learning difficulties were present. All but three of the students used speech to communicate, but in order to help the reader, individual responses have not been acknowledged.

Negotiated learning

Interviewer: Why do you like coming to the unit?
Student: More freedom.
Interviewer: What do you like doing best?
Student: Snooker. Going to college. Student council and Tasks. (From an individual, but typical of other responses).
Interviewer: Tell me about the student council.
Student: We decide what we want to do.... What we need to do.... What we like.
Interviewer: Who decides?
Student: (Indicates the whole group).
Interviewer: Who decides for Harjinder? (A student with profound and multiple learning difficulties).
Student: (Indicates the whole group).
(Harjinder and James had been paired in the previous year in order that James could interpret Harjinder's responses. The group then decided

that everyone should taken the responsibility of interpreting Harjinder's signals).

Interviewer: How can you tell what he wants?
Student: (Makaton sign for 'look').
Interviewer: What does he like?
Student: Massage .... Going out.
Interviewer: What do Harry and Jane do (their teachers).
Student: Help us to change things.

Records of Achievement

When they were asked to comment, the students stated that Records of Achievement:

● 'belonged to them';
● had goals which are jointly set under agreed headings by students and teacher, although in the case of the students with profound and multiple learning difficulties the group was involved in the decisions;
● contained formative and summative information collated by the student, plus examples of work, photographs and certificates;
● included evidence of self-assessment;
● were available for parents to look at;
● were taken by the students into the final annual review meeting;
● provided evidence for a curriculum vitae which every student was helped to compile;
● were taken into the next placement.

The Department of Education and Science (1984) policy statement on Records of Achievement emphasizes that one of the major purposes is 'to provide feedback in order to affect the curriculum, teaching and organisation of the school'.

This section started with a consideration of self-advocacy and Records of Achievement are designed to develop the skills of self-advocacy; the pupil is encouraged to make choices, to be pro-active, to seek change, to maintain control of his learning and to question the system (Marsden, 1991).

The skills of self-advocacy, however, need to be developed and encouraged throughout a pupil's education. The reasons for such a view may be many and varied, but ultimately the priority must be 'that he can voice his opinions on the learning he is receiving'.

The rich data received from pupils and parents should be taken into account in evaluating and developing the curriculum. Both are able and willing, and teachers are accountable to them. We must collaborate.

References

Barton, L. (Ed.) (1989) *Disability and Dependency*. London: Falmer Press.

Broadfoot, P. (1988) 'Profiles and Records of Achievement: a real alternative', *Educational Psychology*, 8, 4, pp. 291–7.

Clare, M. (1990) *Developing Self-Advocacy Skills with People with Disabilities and Learning Difficulties*. London: Further Education Unit.

Cooper, D. and Hersov, J. (1986) *We Can Change the Future*. London: National Bureau for Handicapped Students.

Department of Education and Sciences (1978) *Special Educational Needs: Report of the Committee of Enquiry into the Education of Handicapped Children and Young People* (The Warnock Report). London: HMSO.

Department of Education and Science (1984) *Records of Achievement: A Statement of Policy*. London: HMSO.

Firth, H. and Rapley, M. (1990) *From Acquaintance to Friendship*. Kidderminster: BIMH.

Fowler, W. S. (1990) *Implementing the National Curriculum. The Policy and Practice of the 1988 Education Reform Act*. London: Kegan Paul.

Further Education Unit (1990) *Developing Self Advocacy Skills*. London: FEU.

John, M. (1986) *Disabled Young People Living Independently*. London: British Council of Organisations of Disabled People.

Marsden, S. (1991) 'Records of Achievement. An Alternative Approach for Students with Severe Learning Difficulties'. Unpublished paper, Westhill College.

National Curriculum Council (1990) *Curriculum Guidance 3: The Whole Curriculum*. York: NCC.

Oliver, M. (1989) 'Disability and dependency: A creation of industrial societies', in Barton, L. (Ed.) *Disability and Dependency*. London: Falmer Press.

Russell, M. (1991) 'The Development and Production of Two Records of Achievement'. Unpublished paper, Westhill College.

Staff of Rectory Paddock School (1983) *In Search of a Curriculum* (2nd edn). Sidcup: Robin Wren.

Williams, P. and Shoultz, B. (1982) *We Can Speak for Ourselves*. London: Souvenir Press.

CHAPTER 4

Parents and Professionals

Robert Dolton and John Visser

This chapter gives two perspectives on the relationship between parents and professionals. Robert Dolton offers a parent's view and John Visser outlines ways in which professionals can and should respond to recent legislation.

Oliver's story – a parent's view of the service. *Robert Dolton*

When you have three children aged 8, 6 and 3 and are awaiting the birth of a fourth, you tend to assume that the newcomer will share more than basic humanity and parentage with his or her older sisters and brother. For us, the warning signs of an unusual pregnancy were fairly clear and while there was no reason to expect disability, we were not surprised to discover that our new-born required surgery at birth for duodenal atresia. Our concern was focused on the probability of Oliver's physical survival and we did not speculate on the possibility of intellectual impairment. The interview in the Children's Hospital when we were told that Oliver had Down's syndrome was therefore profoundly shocking as we were forced to recognize the previously ignored indicators of disability.

Oliver was not like the other children: his size, his muscle tone, his inability (or was it refusal?) to make and maintain eye contact were the immediate physical realities which we could not fail to recognize. But as well as coming to terms with the flesh and blood Oliver – what there was of him – there was the dawning recognition that the taken-for-granted rules of welcoming and accepting a newborn baby did not apply. Other people had assumptions, fears and anxieties which they were unable to articulate fully.

For my part, I was involved in the teaching and training of social workers, and soon encountered the force of others' expectations, and was aware of the ease with which I was being enticed into collusion with those who had not even worked through their own responses to disability. Shortly after Oliver's birth and being told that he had Down's syndrome, a health visitor making a home visit commented that I, as a social worker, would know all about mental handicap, and started to leave. I nodded dumbly, not wishing at that point to engage in explanations about my occupation, nor to disclose that of all possible client groups, I was least inclined to work with people with a mental handicap. The latter tendency, derived from a very poor learning experience as a student, was radically altered shortly afterwards on a visit to a student social worker on placement in a mental handicap hospital when I 'saw' people with learning difficulties as people in their own right, for the first time.

Parents of a child with severe learning difficulties find it necessary not only to acquire the knowledge, skill and emotional equilibrium to provide appropriate parenting, but also to undergo a process of induction into socially-constructed responses to disability. For it is to these that individual parents – whatever their blend of personality, social skills, educational background, occupation, social class and racial or ethnic origin – need to contribute. The new parent, like the bereaved, is forced to face a variety of unexpected and formative experiences.

The education service has produced examples of a range of practices, some highly valued, others not so well-received. The family has been supported by many individuals and remembers with gratitude a particular peripatetic teacher. She made regular visits in the first few months to give Oliver physiotherapy and to demonstrate exercises but also provided essential psychological support. Teachers who regularly sent messages home with Oliver at the end of the school day and encouraged parental responses were also valued, as were those other teachers who frequently confirmed his popularity and likeability – even if, at times, they appeared to fly in the face of all the evidence! We enjoyed our involvement over several years with a family-link scheme with a nearby college of education. The aim was to enable students training to be teachers of pupils with severe learning difficulties to gain access to the homes of families with a child with special educational needs and to negotiate ways in which they might become involved. 'Our' students' stance and style (tentative in that none were yet professionally qualified; radical in that they took nothing for granted) was appealing and enabling. We learnt and shared with them, from our first student, who made us feel that she should not be allowed to soil her hands by such basics as toiletting and nappy-changing; our second, who did everything, and became a family friend; and our third who tested Oliver and himself to destruction by taking him on holiday. We were able to share something of our competencies and uncertainties with them, while they, to varying degrees, gave time, affirmation, attention and support.

This sense of affirmation of the family and of its individual members was not, however, a common response. For example, an advisor from a voluntary agency who undertook a home assessment of Oliver at 32 months identified correctly the difficulties we were having as a family with his throwing of objects, and the developmental implications for Oliver himself. One suggestion, to bore a hole in the centre of our pine kitchen table and to insert a wooden post, to which we could attach a ball or other object for Oliver to handle but not use as a projectile, was politely received. It was not acted upon as this was the prized family table, used for all meals, and one of the symbolic emotional centres of the home.

When Oliver was a few months old, we were told of a parents' group to run for 12 sessions and to be set up under the auspices of the Adult Education Service. The planning, input and structuring of the sessions were primarily undertaken by educational psychologists who focused on behavioural approaches to intervention. This did little to contribute to our needs at that time, with the emphasis seemingly on 'doing' – skill development – at the expense of 'being'. We needed the opportunity and the support to get in touch with ourselves.

Barbara Furneaux (1988) commented that,

> There are two main areas in which parents can and should be involved as partners: (1) in intervention and (2) in assessment. At the present time there are many ways in which parents are accepted as partners in intervention techniques . . . less attention has been given to the value of parents as partners in assessment. This is odd, since they are undisputed experts in the knowledge of their own children, the family and their environment (p. 63).

I would question whether they are, or ever can be, 'undisputed experts'. They are certainly in intimate daily contact with their children, and as such can observe the raw behavioural data and may indeed construe and interpret it more accurately than a representative of the education service. Equally, they may collude, or deny, what is apparent to others. They may need a non-family member to validate their experience, to affirm that their interpretation of behaviours or interactions is not idiosyncratic or unduly biased and to confirm that they are going through difficult times, which others have found equally traumatic.

We have valued review meetings at Oliver's schools, the opportunity to comment on our perceptions and views as well as hearing reports from staff. Not infrequently we hear of a new skill or a fresh piece of behaviour and recognize it as something we were aware of some years previously, which leads to some soul-searching. Is this indeed a skill which Oliver has always had, and is now transferring to new situations, or is it that there has been an inadequate sharing of information?

Concern has frequently been expressed about the implementation of the 1981 Education Act and the statementing process. Debate typically occurs when the principle of integration is infringed, or where the Local Education Authority appears satisfied with its segregated special school provision, or where parents believe that their child has been inappropriately placed. While supporting an integrated approach to educational provision, we have always believed that Oliver has such severe impairment as to require placement in a special school, and are satisfied that the recommendation of 7 days a week boarding on transfer to secondary school is appropriate.

Pugh and De'Ath (1989), when discussing pre-school involvement with parents, note that,

> No two parents, no two children, are the same nor will they have the same needs, nor will those needs remain constant over a period of time . . . we met no parents who were not interested in their children's progress, though there were many factors that prevented them becoming as involved in the centre as the nursery workers may have liked. One of these was quite simply whether or not they were working. Many of the assumptions upon which arguments for greater parental involvement are based presume that parents will be free, willing and able to take on the various roles identified by the project (p. 62).

It is vital that involvement is established on the right premise, and that parents are not involved through guilt, collusion or other negative factors. With hindsight, I recognized that very early after Oliver's birth, I colluded with those who assumed I had greater knowledge and expertise than was the case, and I used this to distance myself from my own feelings about having a child with a severe intellectual impairment. Invited very soon to join the executive committee of a voluntary society, formed primarily to meet the needs of parents of children with a mental handicap, I found the atmosphere stultifying and not conducive to the exploration of my still-inarticulated feelings. Cast prematurely in the role of 'an expert parent', I found myself on campaigning bodies, required to speak publicly, and to make policy decisions. I was saved from myself by a group of students who, after a teaching session, thanked me for my input, and then astutely asked why I sounded more like a professional than a parent. This salutary incident started to bring me to my senses, but it was sad that no 'professional' had thought to assess my need before that time.

Part of the need for us has been to acquire the skill of learning to cope with a child with severe learning difficulties while affirming his full humanity and his right to as full and as normal a life as possible. This has been demonstrated by a narrowing of horizons, a foreshortening of expectations. No longer do we fantasize that Oliver might have gainful employment as an adult, nor do we think that he will ever be able to live independently. But we do recognize the importance of encouraging the development of independence and life skills in so far as this increases his quality of life, and we are conscious of how determined his teachers are in attempting to implement these aims.

Comments have been made on the pressures experienced because we are white and middle class; we sometimes reflect on how we would have coped had 'many of the key concepts and philosophies underpinning community care policies...' not been '...inherently white or Eurocentric in thier assumptions' (Booth, 1990, p. 11). What would our perceptions of the education services be if Oliver and we had been Black?

Legislation does not change parents' needs. *John Visser*

On a warm December day a young man was driving to his in-laws to share the joy of having become a father for the first time. Later that day he drove back to the hospital to visit his wife and son. He walked into the ward to find his wife looking far from happy, for their baby had been taken away to intensive care. A physical defect had been diagnosed and during a consultation with the doctor, who was quiet and pleasant in her approach, the problem was discussed. As she spoke, the father realized that the condition described was the one from which he himself suffered. Was it his fault? What was the prognosis for the child? Would their son survive and be able to live a full and happy life? Why had it happened to them? These and many other fears flashed through his mind.

The present writer was that young man and the experience provides useful insights into Oliver's parents' responses at the interview in the Children's Hospital. The birth of a baby arouses feelings normally associated with our sense of worth and self-esteem and, when a child is 'not perfect', these feelings are challenged. The anxieties of many parents are quickly displaced by an ability to 'cope' and they try to become as 'normal' a family as possible. For some the task becomes insuperable; others see their child as 'handicapped'; and a minority believe their child to be 'able' with 'some disabilities'!

It is at this critical point that parents meet a range of professionals. The experience described by Oliver's father is by no means unique and it has been recounted many times both by researchers and parents (Wolfendale, 1984; Dyson, 1987). It is a truism that the bringer of bad tidings is seldom remembered with affection; it is, however, sad that parents often report that the professional who first made them aware of their child's disability was insensitive, abrupt and patronizing. Similarly, the feeling of isolation that results is not uncommon and many parents have passed similar comments to those made by Oliver's. The assumption made by the health worker that professionals who work in the caring services can handle the situation is reinforced by the literature (Wolfendale, 1984). On the other hand, there is evidence to suggest that if parents appear inarticulate, the professionals will assume that they are unable to understand and either patronize or possibly ignore them completely. Neither approach is helpful in establishing positive relationships and it is essential for any professional to appreciate that all parents are uncertain and genuinely concerned. The initial diagnosis must mark the beginning of a significant partnership and it is quite unacceptable for parents to have to complain of 'a lack of meaningful contact with professionals' (McConachie, 1986). There is evidence to suggest that professional organizations and schools have attempted to rectify some of the difficulties (Chapter 8) but it was the Warnock Report (DES, 1978) which focused attention on the importance of worthwhile partnerships. The Report sees parents as essential educators of their children, particularly in the early years, and working with parents has become a guiding principle. 'Parents as partners' became the slogan in schools and teachers incorporated it as a working axiom. Mittler and Mittler (1982) examined this approach and provided guidance for professionals in enhancing their skills as well as in writing their policy documents.

Parental rights are fundamental to the working of the 1981 Education Act. The legislation, based upon the recommendations of the Warnock Report, gives parents a central role in the education of their children. They are regarded as important throughout the process of ascertaining special educational needs and their position is brought into sharp focus when a statement is required. Parents can initiate the process, although it is more usual for the professionals associated with pre-school provision to notify the LEA of the need to make a statement. Statementing can be seen as cumbersome for professionals and ponderously bureaucratic in its operation. It can be argued, however, that it is essentially an effective mechanism for guaranteeing that parents are at least involved in determining the provisions made to meet their child's special educational needs. The legislation, in this respect, protects the natural rights of parents and it is important to remember that they have not always been consulted. Until 1970 their children did not have a legal right to education if they had been deemed ineducable by a school medical officer and it was not until the implementation of the 1981 Education Act, in April 1983, that parents were normally consulted about placements recommended for their children. Under the Act, parents must be fully consulted at all stages of statementing, whoever is the initiator, and they have the right of access to all evidence used to determine a statement of educational need. It should be understood, however, that the document is concerned solely with educational and not medical or social needs, and that these factors may only be taken into account when they impinge on the education of the child. Once written and agreed to by the parents and the LEA, a statement becomes a legally-binding contract.

The required consultation is a prerequisite for any meaningful and realistic statement as parents have unique insights into their children's strengths, weaknesses and achievements. Statements which depend solely on the views of professionals will inevitably be partial and inaccurate.

The debate on integration within a mainstream school, or separation in a special school, is of concern to both professionals and parents. The correct placement for an individual child may not, in all circumstances, be available and unfortunately compromises have to be made. The statementing process, by requiring needs to be explicitly stated, should enable parents and professionals to arrive at the 'best' placement. If there is a continuum of need it must be matched by a continuum of provision. Professionals should guard against a child being placed where there is a space in a resource on purely financial criteria. Every placement should be based solely on each child's needs.

Circular 22/89 (DES, 1989) clearly defines the procedure for arriving at a statement. The process begins with a notification to the parents that the LEA intends to initiate this course of action. The parents then have 29 days in which to acknowledge the letter and to raise objections. The parents must be given the name of the contact person appointed by the local authority, usually referred to as the 'named person'. He or she should ensure that the parents are fully involved, particularly in the collection of evidence utilized to create the statement, which may include their own data. All this information should be used to write Sections 3 and 4 of the statement covering needs and curriculum provision. Section 5, relating to placement, is written as a consequence of these assessments. Thus the statement is based upon the educational needs of the child and is 'needs-led'. The reality may be that the professionals fail to follow this procedure and produce 'resources-led' statements determined by the provisions readily available. Under Circular 22/89 (DES, 1989) professionals are obliged to ensure that parents are fully consulted and aware of their rights, including the right to appeal, under the 1981 Act. Where necessary, voluntary agencies must also be informed.

Statementing is not without its problems. Sometimes an inordinate amount of time is spent in preparing the document and often children are placed before the necessary process has been completed. Although this may not be directly in contravention of the law it is certainly against the spirit of the 1981 Act and Circular 22/89 (DES, 1989), which indicate that the whole process should be completed within six months.

The 1988 Education Reform Act (DES, 1988) has posed further problems for teachers of children with severe learning difficulties. In its current form it is a two-edged sword. Its major strength is the notion of an entitlement curriculum. Legislation in the 1970s ensured that children with severe learning difficulties were brought into education; in the 1988 Education Act they are guaranteed an education which is universal, broad and balanced. Thus the particular advantages of the Act have been the opportunities that it offers for a re-examination of the curriculum previously delivered, and the questioning of the narrow focus on basic and social skills. The entitlement curriculum presents new challenges to provide and deliver an education which broadens a pupil's knowledge, experience and understanding. As a direct result, with help from parents, the boundaries to what children with severe learning difficulties are able to achieve will continue to be extended.

The implementation of a broad and balanced curriculum under the legislation within the Act has, however, caused problems, the most serious of which is the rigid linking of key stages and programmes of study to the ages of pupils. For pupils with severe learning difficulties the result is an age-related rather than a stage-related curriculum and therefore programmes of study are determined by age and not, as is appropriate, by the stage of the child's development. Such a mismatch will continue to result in additional disadvantages and, unfortunately, the Department of Education and Science and the Secretary of State for Education seem disinclined to address the issue. In a democracy, elected politicians are accountable for education, and other public services, and must be sensitive to the need for change. A partnership of professionals and parents can form a powerful lobby, calculated to ensure that problems are addressed and ways forward found.

The National Curriculum prescribes the core and foundation subjects, the cross-curricular themes and the extra-curricula areas to be undertaken by any school. Although it has been argued that it is inappropriate for children with severe learning difficulties and that they should be allowed to opt out, such a development needs to be seen as reprehensible and retrograde. A broad and balanced curriculum, on which the National Curriculum is based, needs to be delivered in ways which enable all pupils to learn and which demonstrates to parents that all their children's needs are adequately provided for. Failure to deliver could result in the removal of pupils with severe learning difficulties from the education system as it could be claimed that they are no longer in receipt of education as defined by the 1988 Act. It should be reiterated that the National Curriculum is only part of the curriculum and not the whole.

Oliver's entitlement to education was the result of a long struggle by both parents and professionals. It must be unacceptable to exempt him and other pupils with severe learning difficulties from their entitlement, and creating for them a separate and separatist curriculum. They must stay within the National Curriculum, which is flexible enough to meet the needs of each individual child.

The Act provides four ways in which a child's entitlement may be changed: orders, disapplication, exemption and modification.

Whichever is used, pupils are still entitled to a broad and balanced curriculum covered by the ten subjects and the cross-curriculum themes of the National Curriculum (Section 1 of the 1988 Education Act).

Orders are issued under Section 4 of the Act by the Secretary of State and are recommended to him by the National Curriculum Council. An example of the flexibility of the system is demonstrated by the changes made to Attainment Target 5: Handwriting, which ensures that children who need mechanical means to represent their written expression are no longer required to reach this target.

'Disapplication' is the term used to indicate that an individual pupil is not required to undertake specified areas of the National Curriculum. Such a step threatens the position of the pupil within the education system. All documents which discuss the term, whether from the Department of Education and Science, the National Curriculum Council, the School's Examination and Assessment Council or the Secretary of State, caution against this procedure and stress that its use will be 'rare' (see, in particular, NCC, 1989).

'Exemption', at times, seems to be synonymous with 'disapplication' and may be interpreted as applying only to a specific subject or its attainment targets. Its use may also be rare, but it can be applied to some children for a limited period in relation, for example, to a modern foreign language. 'Modification' is used in relation to attainment targets, to levels within them and to programmes of study.

Disapplications, exemptions and modifications can only be implemented after a Statement under Section 18 or the use of Temporary Directions under Section 19 of the Act.

Despite recent changes in legislation, some of the needs of parents have yet to be met. Although good practice has increased and parents have been given the opportunity to play a central role in the education of their children, full partnership is not universal. Professionals must be encouraged to consider effective ways of communicating with parents and of ensuring that the implementation of the legislation depends upon partnership and mutual understanding. These aims can only be achieved if in-service education for all professionals includes opportunities to acquire the skills of collaborative working, and their value is clearly articulated by Oliver's parents. Unfortunately, initial teacher education programmes specializing in work with pupils with severe learning difficulties have been discontinued and the opportunities that were offered to Oliver and his students are no longer available. In-service programmes must include ways of meeting such

50

needs. It must not be assumed that teachers of mainstream pupils have the in-depth experience and knowledge of the difficulties experienced by Oliver's family (Atkin *et al.*, 1988).

School policy statements must emphasize, and practice should demonstrate, the benefits to be gained when parents are partners. Some schools use a joint team of parents and teachers to prepare these and other documents. The training programme prepared by Charnock *et al.* (1991) makes salutary reading, as it demonstrates both the arrogance and biased assumptions of insensitive professionals.

Sadly, Oliver's story indicates the unfeeling way in which many professionals continue to work. The spate of legislation over the past 15 years has done little to meet the needs of parents but has indicated ways of achieving good practice. It is through a relationship of mutual understanding between parents and professionals that a true partnership will emerge. With it will come meaningful benefits for pupils with severe learning difficulties through the setting of realistic educational goals within statements and a clearer identification of the constraints under which professionals work.

References

Atkin, J., Bastiani, J. and Goode, J. (1988) *Listening to Parents*. London: Croom Helm.

Booth, T. (Ed.) (1990) *Better Lives: Changing Services for People with Learning Difficulties*. Sheffield: Joint Unit for Social Services Research.

Charnock, S., Dennis, P., Lang, M. and Osman, J. (1991) 'Working with families: developing a partnership between parents and professionals in the mental handicap services', *Mental Handicap*, 19, March, pp. 11–13.

Department of Education and Science (1978) *Special Educational Needs: Report of the Committee of Enquiry into the Education of Handicapped Children and Young People* (The Warnock Report). London: HMSO.

Department of Education and Science (1981) *Education Act*. London: HMSO.

Department of Education and Science (1988) *Education Reform Act*. London: HMSO.

Department of Education and Science (1989) *Assessments and Statements of Special Educational Needs: Procedures within Education, Health and Social Services*, Circular 22/89. London: HMSO.

Dyson, S. (1987) *Mental Handicap: Dilemmas of Parent–Professional Relations*. London: Croom Helm.

Furneaux, B. (1988) *Special Parents*. Milton Keynes: Open University Press.

McConachie, H. (1986) *Parents and Young Mentally Handicapped Children*. London: Croom Helm.

Mittler, P. and Mittler, H. (1982) *Partnership with Parents*. Stratford: NCSE.

National Curriculum Council (1989) *Curriculum Guidance 2: A Curriculum for All*. York: NCC.

Pugh, G. and De'Ath, E. (Eds) (1989) *Working towards Partnership in the Early Years*. London: National Children's Bureau.

Wolfendale, S. (1984) *Parental Participation in Children's Development and Education*. New York: Gordon & Breach.

PART TWO

CHAPTER 5

Influences on Curriculum Design and on Assessment

Penny Lacey, Beryl Smith and Christina Tilstone

The legal right to education for pupils with severe learning difficulties, brought about by the Education (Handicapped Children) Act of 1970, presented a dilemma for the staff of the new special schools. Previously, within the Training Centres controlled by Local Health Authorities, formal educational curriculum planning and implementation had not been obligatory. Some Centres had, however, adopted a diluted nursery/infant model which had proved ill-suited to the diverse needs of pupils. From 1970, teachers from both mainstream and schools for pupils with moderate learning difficulties were attracted by the challenge of teaching pupils who had formerly been excluded from the education system. Thus ideas from mainstream and special schools were combined with existing Training Centre practices and new curriculum frameworks began to emerge. Innovations reflected the general process of social, economic and political change which was influencing the design and development of the curriculum in all sectors of education. Gordon and Lawton (1978) provide a useful and detailed study of these influences on the history of curriculum change in the nineteenth and twentieth centuries.

The definition of a curriculum in mainstream education in the 1960s was:

> all the learning which is planned and guided by the school whether it is carried on in groups or individually inside or outside the school (Kerr, 1968, p. 16.

In practice it was accepted as valid in schools for pupils with severe learning difficulties as the potency of 'hidden learning' was not fully appreciated and formal timetabled courses of study were regarded as essential. Fortunately teachers of pupils with severe learning difficulties began to be influenced by the more penetrating definition developed by Tansley and Gulliford (1960). They suggested the curriculum was composed of two closely linked and interdependent parts which offered

> opportunities for vital experience, creative expression and the development of social awareness, at the same time allows efficient teaching of the basic subjects and helps each child to learn more effectively (p. 101).

The two parts formed a central core of basic work on language and numeracy, and a periphery of additional knowledge about the environment, creative and aesthetic activities, and practical interests. The various elements were not considered static, however, for as the child achieved a command of the essential skills in the core area, he used them to broaden his experience in other areas.

Almost 20 years after the publication of Tansley and Gulliford's work, Ainscow and Tweddle (1979) developed a more precise definition of these elements. They called them the 'closed or open areas' of the curriculum: the closed area was concerned with mastery learning expressed in precise behavioural objectives; the open component exposed the pupil to experiences which would allow for the generalization of skills obtained in the closed area. Although, in theory, teachers saw this as an improvement on the Tansley and Gulliford model, in practice, many special schools concentrated on the closed area and delivered a narrow and often unpalatable skills-based curriculum. However, some basic agreement was developing in schools about the essential nature of communication and independent living skills. Wilson (1981) in a Schools Council project based on a two-day seminar, 'to consider the curriculum in special schools', emphasized that skills were relevant across the whole curriculum and had

> a better chance of developing within the framework of a broadly based curriculum than by a narrow concentration of skills in isolation (p. 15).

This notion of a broadly-based curriculum was particularly trouble-some for teachers of children with severe learning difficulties, as slow developers require additional time for learning. Time was, and still is, a major limiting factor in curriculum development. Grappling with this constraint in the 1970s, many schools adopted what Brennan (1985) calls the 'instructional approach' to curriculum design. He states that the curriculum content should be organized according to a hierarchy of importance into three categories of instructional priority: those that:

> must be learned. This is the core of the curriculum the imperative essential minimum to be mastered by the learners;
>
> should be learned. Content in this category is to be learned only if the 'must' category is firmly established;
>
> could be learned. To be attempted only by learners who master the content of the 'must' and 'should' categories (pp. 67–8).

The constraints of time on the curriculum became even more important as this model was widely adopted. In general, in the early 1970s pupils entered school at 5 and left at 16. Brennan comments that, within these limits, it is impossible for schools to present pupils with every learning experience which would be beneficial to them as adolescents leaving school. The Warnock Report found evidence to suggest that pupils with severe learning difficulties continue to learn after the age of 16, but it required action by a group of parents in Oxfordshire to remind Local Education Authorities of the Report's recommendation that, where it is in their best interests, pupils with special educational needs should be allowed to receive education beyond the statutory school leaving age (Hurt, 1988). Also, in order to overcome the constraints of time, pupils have been admitted to special schools at an increasingly early age and the recognized importance of early intervention has strengthened this trend. Unfortunately, this tendency has resulted in 2-year-old children often being admitted to environments ill-suited to their needs.

The Report recognized that the tasks and skills learned by pupils with severe learning difficulties have to be analysed precisely, and that the 'setting of small, clearly defined incremental objectives for individual children is a necessary part of the programme planning' (DES, 1978, p. 221). The approach to education taken by the Warnock Committee and others (Crawford, 1980; Leeming et al., 1979; Mittler, 1979) was dependent on a behavioural approach to curriculum planning. Encouraged by the development of the techniques of behaviour modification for people with mental handicap in the USA and Britain in the 1960s, a behavioural framework for the curriculum emerged. This framework was extended and developed by Gardner et al. (1983) to provide a skills analysis model (SAM) of curriculum design. SAM, which has had a profound influence on the curriculum of schools for pupils with severe learning difficulties, uses six basic steps in its development:

1. Identify CORE AREAS of the curriculum.
2. Subdivide core areas into their COMPONENT PARTS.
3. Write TARGETS for each component.
4. ORDER targets.
5. Write PROGRAMMES designed to teach target skills.
6. Devise an on-going ASSESSMENT and RECORD KEEPING system.
   (p. 25)

The model, which requires the teacher to define the targets in terms of behavioural outcomes, the conditions under which the learning will take place, and the criteria for acceptable performance, is concerned with product. It has been questioned for its limiting effects (Goddard, 1983; McConkey, 1981; Smith, 1989; Smith *et al.*, 1983). However, its strength lies in the emphasis on a school-based, school-focused curriculum, developed by the staff for their own pupils. It requires, and has successfully helped to achieve, a whole-school approach to curriculum planning and implementation.

Also developed in the early 1980s was a model reported by Wilson (1981), stemming from practice in a school for pupils with moderate learning difficulties. The framework went beyond the skills-based and considered attitudes and experiences. Teachers of pupils with severe learning difficulties found it appealing, as the fostering of self-confidence, personal initiative and consideration for others was often neglected in a pre-determined objectives-based curriculum. Although teachers were well aware that experiences alone, no matter how rich or varied, are not sufficient unless designed and structured to reflect each child's developmental level, they were finding that, contrary to previous opinion, most children could learn incidentally. The exposure of pupils to aesthetic, creative and social experiences was necessary and desirable.

The way in which a curriculum is structured depends upon the priorities teachers select for their pupils, and requires an agreed philosophical framework. Coupe and Porter (1986) introduced a two-part curriculum framework which many schools have found a useful extension of the Skills Analysis Model. As with SAM, this model determines the objectives of the curriculum in terms of behaviours, but encourages staff to make explicit the ideology behind their chosen aims, and also to consider the normal developmental stages through which children pass, as 'goals'. Goals are 'a combination of developmental behaviours, skills analysis and appropriate environmental influences' (p. 20) which take the form of developmental sequences. The authors give the following example:

CORE AREA: MOTOR DEVELOPMENT
Sub-core area: fine motor development
Goals: 1. fine motor checklist 1 to 12 months
       2. related fine motor activities 1 to 12 months
       3. fine motor checklist 12–30 months
       4. fine motor checklist 30–60 months
       5. pre-writing 1 to 7.
(p. 18)

Ouvry (1987), in her curriculum model for children with profound and multiple learning difficulties, uses developmental areas as a prerequisite for defining core areas of the curriculum. Physical, perceptual, intellectual, personal and social development lead into the core areas of movement and perceptual motor; sensory awareness; cognitive skills and communication; and independence. This is a valuable model as it is primarily concerned with enabling pupils to gain a comprehensive understanding of their world of people, objects and events.

McConkey (1981) sees 'understanding' as the essential element in knowledge, and emphasizes that it is more valuable than the acquisition of facts and skills. It can be the direct result of process-(rather than product-) centred teaching and may enable pupils to develop concepts. His research has influenced advances in interactive approaches to curriculum delivery, with their emphasis on problem-solving and decision-making. The approach has gained greater recognition through the recent work of Glenn (1988), Nind and Hewett (1988), Smith (1988) and Watson (1990) who emphasize the need to structure the environment in order to facilitate self-directed learning and to promote cognitive processes. These innovations have encouraged many teachers to reconsider the content of their curricula and to provide opportunities for their pupils to take responsibility for their own learning.

Technical and Vocational Education (TVE) has also had a significant effect on curriculum development. Introduced by the government in 1982 as a pilot initiative, it quickly gained popularity and is now a potent force in secondary and tertiary education. Its initial aim was to bridge the gap between school and work by providing relevant programmes of vocational and general education, as a preparation for employment. The consequent curriculum developments were largely technical or vocational in emphasis, although 'often problem-solving and personal effectiveness was included' (Cooper, 1987). Cooper adds that TVE(I) has provided funding for specific initiatives such as work experience, information technology, increased opportunities for integration, broader curriculum options, and opportunities to explore a range of educational environments. It has undoubtedly helped people with special learning difficulties to take a more active part in the life of the community and, at the same time, has identified effective methods of curriculum delivery.

An important influence on curriculum design has been the increase in the numbers of children from ethnic and cultural minorities in schools for pupils with severe learning difficulties. Teachers now recognize that all aspects of the curriculum need to reflect differences in language, culture and origin. Chapter 6 focuses on aspects of the multi-cultural curriculum.

The 1988 Education Reform Act has also resulted in radical changes to the character of the curriculum previously evolved in schools for pupils with severe learning difficulties. Teachers were, therefore, in the difficult position of having to fight for their pupils' inclusion in something which initially bore little resemblance to their own school's curriculum. On a closer analysis of the programmes of study, teachers have found that their existing curricula contain much of what is suggested at Levels 1 and 2 in the core subjects.

Teachers of pupils with severe learning difficulties throughout England and Wales have documented their progress in accessing the National Curriculum for their pupils (East Sussex SLD Schools, 1990; Fagg *et al.*, 1990; West Midlands Monitoring Group SLD, 1989; 1990; 1991); other special educators have expressed their concerns (Staff of Tyne Green School, 1991; Ware, 1990). In order to help teachers of pupils with severe learning difficulties to implement the National Curriculum in the core subjects, the National Curriculum Council has funded a team of teachers whose brief is to provide examples of effective practice.

Many schools have blended their own curricula and the National Curriculum and have managed to preserve those elements which meet the specific needs of their pupils and are outside the National Curriculum itself. Teachers have modified the titles of their core areas in line with the core and foundation subjects but it should be stressed that social competence, including feeding, dressing and toileting is no less important since the implementation of the National Curriculum.

The National Curriculum also requires teachers to undertake a rigorous examination of their existing practices. The Council's

Curriculum Guidance 3 (1990) encourages school staff to review and evaluate their own curriculum through the preparation of a school development plan. Schools are legally bound to ensure that the curriculum is broad and balanced – an issue of concern to HMI for pupils with severe, and complex learning difficulties (DES, 1990a).

Unfortunately, as the emphasis in early National Curriculum documents was on attainment targets, teachers at first did not appreciate the potential of the programmes of study. Although the programmes themselves provide clear guidelines for the planning of schemes of work, the attainment targets appear inappropriate to many teachers. It is not the intention of the authors to underestimate the difficulties of adapting or modifying the National Curriculum in order to meet the disparate needs of pupils for whom it was not originally designed. Wedell (1990) emphasizes the potential dangers: 'It is not easy to decide when modifications to attainment targets turn into formal modifications and disapplications' (p. 8). The Task Group on Assessment and Testing (DES, 1988) clearly stated that assessment should be the responsibility of the teachers and that it should take place in classrooms as an integral part of the teaching/learning process. Unfortunately, the government have seen fit to reduce the emphasis on teacher assessment and have allowed standard assessment tests to take precedence.

Gipps (1990) argues that 'assessment is, after all, a tool for teachers, to be used for the benefit of children' (p. 99) and sees it as part of the learning process. It is important to consider the background to assessment for pupils with severe learning difficulties in order to set the implications of the National Curriculum in context.

Assessment in schools for pupils with severe learning difficulties

Special schools may, with some justification, claim to have been forerunners in developing the current concept of educational assessment which considers assessment to be part of a circular educational process incorporating assessment, programme planning, delivery, re-assessment and evaluation. In this process, assessment informs decisions on appropriate teaching objectives and teaching strategies. The reason for assessment in education is basically to provide a guide to appropriate education, not to judge the child on his performance.

Gathering data by means of norm-referenced assessment

The assessment techniques of the earlier part of this century were mainly concerned with assessing an individual's intellectual ability relative to that of his peers. A number of tasks were presented and the total number of successes, by defined criteria, were added to give a score – thus a measure of the quantity of intellectual development was obtained. Such assessment may be of a global variety in which a score is given for overall development (Thorndike *et al.*, 1985; Wechsler, 1974) or may describe performance in a particular area (Lowe and Costello, 1973; Reynell, 1977). Although it was usual to relate the pupil's score to that of his age peers and obtain an intelligence quotient, performance on some tests can be described as a mental age or developmental age rather than as a quotient. Used in this way, scales such as those of Griffiths (1954) or Bayley (1969) give developmental scores in the areas of language, motor and adaptive behaviour. Such developmental-age scores are of greater value than a quotient since they give a description of the child's particular level of achievement, rather than his achievement in relation to other children.

However, there are considerable drawbacks in gathering data for educational assessment by means of these instruments. They are quantitative assessment instruments and the score is the total number of successes gained. Similar total scores may be obtained as a result of very different types of performance. Various learning difficulties demand specific educational programmes but a total score gives no indication of these requirements. The other objections to the use of quantitative instruments include the fact that such tests can discriminate against individuals of specific race and social class, since the items have usually been standardized on specific populations. For children with severe learning difficulties, scores were often calculated approximately from those obtained on a population whose members were within the 'normal' range of sensory and motor ability. In addition, such tests were usually administered by educational psychologists who may have received limited training in the area of severe learning difficulties.

As a result of social and educational changes and increased understanding of the importance of individual differences in development, the wide range of quantitative tests, whether used in a norm-referenced fashion or not, tend to be rejected. It may be that quantitative assessment still has a useful role to play in the screening and identification of children with severe learning difficulties, in the identification of specific sensory and motor handicaps and for research purposes. It does not, however, provide adequate information for individual programme planning.

Certainly the Task Group for Assessment and Testing stated that National Curriculum tests should not be comparative, i.e., they should not be related to an outside norm, or have reference to averages of performances in a standardized manner. It is likely, therefore, that norm-referenced testing will become obsolete in assessment in special schools in the foreseeable future.

Gathering data by means of criterion-referenced assessment

The use of criterion-referenced assessment has undoubtedly benefited education for children with severe learning difficulties. Teachers have been encouraged to define suitable objectives for each child, to keep records and to pass on relevant information on a child's progress or lack of it, and also to clarify their own thinking on the nature of the curriculum. The pupil's performance is assessed in various areas, such as social development, language, cognition, motor skills and visuo-motor ability and by means of check-lists of items. These items are sequentially arranged descriptions of behaviours, characteristic of development in each area.

Criterion-referenced instruments are often linked to instructions on what material to present, in what fashion, and the response requirements that determine whether or not the pupil is meeting the criteria for that particular behaviour. Examples of such instruments are the Portage Early Education Programme (White and Cameron, 1987) and Early Learning Skills Analysis (Ainscow and Tweddle, 1984).

In addition to using published criterion-referenced material, staff of many schools devise their own. The behaviours which the child demonstrates in a satisfactory manner are not added up, as with the former quantitative type of assessment, but indicate what he can do and what he needs to be taught next. Children are 'base-lined' in each area by the identification of the skills they possess and those they lack. Programme planning is aimed at teaching immediately above the level at which the child shows competence. Re-assessment follows the same model and in this way a close account may be kept of a pupil's progress, appropriate learning objectives may be determined and comparisons of stages in an individual child's development can be drawn.

The Schools' Examination and Assessment Council's (SEAC, 1990) *Guidance on Teacher Assessment and Collection of Evidence* endorses the use by special schools of criterion-referenced tests as being in accordance with National Curriculum Teacher Assessment Guidelines. Testing is described as a means of identifying what has been successfully learned in order to determine subsequent stages in planning for groups and individuals.

Problems, however, may stem from an over-reliance on criterion-referenced assessment, of which teachers are becoming increasingly aware. These include the self-limiting nature of the items; each new check-list is largely derived from those already in existence, which may or may not be descriptions of behaviours crucial in development or arranged in a valid developmental sequence. Acceptance of existing descriptions raises the question of whether progressive developments provide suitable or relevant landmarks for the assessment of children with severe learning difficulties. In addition, there is the problem of testing what is taught. If lists of criterion-referenced behaviours are used for assessment and also as curriculum documents, as often happens, they merely verify that a particular skill has been taught. Education can become focused on the teaching of such specific skills or behaviours to the exclusion of the development of knowledge and understanding.

Gathering data by means of dynamic assessment

This method is not widely used in schools in Britain, although it is not new. Dynamic assessment is concerned with the assessment of mental processes, rather than mental products, and ways in which these processes may be developed. In the Soviet Union a form of dynamic assessment, based on Vygotsky's theory of the Zone of Proximal Development has long been used in the assessment of children with learning difficulties. It aims to identify the processes involved in a successful or an unsuccessful performance. Using the information gathered, teaching programmes are concentrated on the zone preceding the next important landmark in development. Feuerstein's 'Learning Potential Assessment' is also concerned with assessing the process of learning, and although probably more suited for use with pupils with moderate to mild learning difficulties, it is claimed to be of value with some children with severe learning difficulties. Assessment then leads to remediation via the 'Instrumental Enrichment Programme' (Feuerstein *et al.*, 1979).

There has been considerable interest in the United States in methods of dynamic assessment which emphasize the individual's potential for growth, and focus on processes involved in learning. Campione (1989) describes investigations of 'assisted assessment' in which rather than assessing what the child can already do, the educator aims to detect ways in which interventions can be designed to improve the quality of processes rather than products. When a pupil encounters difficulties, the teacher measures the amount and type of help required to achieve competence, an approach which appears to promise more than that of merely deciding upon appropriate objectives.

Other considerations in the assessment of pupils with severe learning difficulties

The Warnock Report lists four requirements for effective assessment: that parents must be closely involved; that it should aim to discover how a child learns and responds over a period of time; that it must include investigations of any aspect of the child's performance which is causing concern; and that family circumstances must be taken into account (DES, 1978, 4.29–32). The Report might well have added a fifth requirement stipulating that assessment should meet changing concepts of education for children with severe learning difficulties. Techniques which assess process in a number of developmental areas and which relate levels of performance to particular educational intervention need to be evolved. An example of need is seen in the area of language development. Research into process in young 'normal' children has uncovered much information which is of value in special education (Harris, 1990; Wells, 1985). At the moment language assessment is largely carried out by means of its products and thus new insights to inform educational programmes are not obtained.

A further changing concept of special education is that the child with severe learning difficulties does not benefit from being 'compartmentalized' (Coupe and Porter, 1986). Undue attention to separate areas of behaviour may result in the inhibition of beneficial cross-fertilization which occurs when parallel developments are encouraged. The special education intervention strategy of separating curriculum into areas may be disadvantageous, in that it acts against one set of behaviours being of service to another. In order to link assessment into a more synchronized curriculum, we need to know far more about the child's parallel explorations and the conditions for the establishment of specific developments. There is, for example, considerable evidence that development in play and language are related (Hill and Nicolich, 1981) but different instruments are used to assess each area. Le Normand (1986) has started to develop integrated assessment techniques by focusing on developmental trends in symbolic play, cognitive organization of language, and pragmatic organization within a play situation. This form of assessment contributes to the diagnosis of functional discrepancies in children with severe learning difficulties but, more importantly, to the planning of appropriate and significant activities which stimulate developments in the 'whole child'.

It has been feared that the assessment and testing of children within the National Curriculum would 'compartmentalize' individual pupils as the remit of TGAT was to 'show what a pupil has learned and mastered' (V-24, DES, 1988). Fortunately, however, the Group approached the project creatively and insisted that it was essential to build on existing good practice. Assessment was therefore regarded as an integral part of the whole educational process, in which a balance between precision and detail on the one hand, and an overall grouping of the ideas, understanding and achievements of pupils on the other, was achieved. This positive use of assessment was based on four criteria. The first, discussed above, is criterion-referenced; the remainder are the criteria of formation, of moderation and of progression. Thus, if criterion-referenced assessment gives direct information about a pupil's achievement in relation to objectives, the formative provides a basis for decisions about a pupil's further needs. The moderated assessments enable comparisons to be made across classes by pupils, parents and teachers. Progressive assessments indicate expected routes of educational development.

The Report goes on to consider the purpose of assessment:

- formative, so that the positive achievements of a pupil may be recognised and discussed and the appropriate steps may be planned;
- diagnostic, through which learning difficulties may be scrutinised and classified so that appropriate remedial help and guidance can be provided;
- summative, for the recording of the overall achievements of a pupil in a systematic way;
- evaluative, by means of which some aspects of the work of a school, an LEA or other discrete part of the Educational Service can be assessed and/or reported upon (V-23, DES, 1988).

National assessment

TGAT's recommendations emphasized the importance of both standardized and teacher assessment, but unfortunately, recent government policies appear to undervalue the latter. The requirements, however, for assessment by means of Standard Assessment Tests (SATs) at ages 7, 11, 14 and 16 have not, at the time of writing, been made clear for pupils with severe learning difficulties. SATs are being piloted in selected special schools, but it appears that they are generally considered to be unsuitable, in their present form, for many pupils with special educational needs. Teacher assessment, however, has produced less problems, and offers a range of opportunities for further development in both special and mainstream schools. The work in progress has already demonstrated the potential for further expansion in the techniques used for the collection of evidence, the management of assessment, and the involvement of pupils in their own assessment and in the development of school policies.

The collection of evidence

Pupils in special schools are involved in a wide variety of educational activities and it is therefore essential to ensure that the evidence for learning can be expressed in a variety of forms. Oral responses to stimuli, the production of artifacts, the demonstration of social skills and the performance of dramatic sequences must be seen as exact and admissible evidence. The collection of evidence on the outcomes of pupils' learning must be preceded by an adequate explanation to the pupils themselves of the criteria to be used. Hughes (1986) suggested that a teacher who, for example, gives children farm animals to count, must make it clear to them that counting is required and that random or creative play is not acceptable on this occasion. It is difficult to make criteria clear to pupils with profound and multiple learning difficulties, but the use of limited choices, demonstrations and examples needs to be considered.

As has already been suggested, assessment is much more than the usually accepted check-lists of the outcomes of learning. The danger is that the pre-determined collection of evidence may lead to the elimination of the unexpected or the exciting. It is particularly difficult for a teacher to record what is actually happening during a spontaneous discussion with a pupil or between pupils involved in mutual interaction or negotiations in a problem-solving exercise.

Consequently, the teacher benefits from an open approach to the evidence collected. In setting up a situation designed to reveal evidence of learning, she may include a set of prompts which can be used to direct her observations and determine her questions. *The Primary Language Record* (Barrs *et al.*, 1988) is a good example of this technique. The guidelines suggest that all modes of talk (oral expression) should be recorded in diary form. The example prompts are aimed at primary school children with a better level of communication than is usually demonstrated by pupils with severe learning difficulties, but more suitable prompts can be substituted to suit the level of ability and the evidence being sought. Teachers have begun to experiment with recording schedules using prompts and some interesting work has been noted by Laycock (1990). Teachers in the Borough of Merton have used notebooks containing check-lists of areas to be observed and these are already proving successful.

The accepted method of teaching and learning in classrooms for pupils with severe learning difficulties has been to teach and then to test each individual on each small step. It must seem like an endless set of hoops to be jumped through. Many writers have been critical of this way of working (McConkey, 1981), and practice in many classrooms no longer emphasizes the importance of learning isolated, and largely mechanical, skills, but is concerned with the development of real understanding. However, it must be recognized that work within a tightly prescribed programme is easier to record than those processes and products which reflect individual knowledge. It is always more difficult to demonstrate the understanding of a concept than the mastery of a skill or the repetition of facts. The attainment targets of the National Curriculum are written in terms which are probably less precise than those of a curriculum influenced by prescriptive behavioural objectives and should encourage teachers to use more open forms of assessment, dependent upon observation rather than direct testing.

Managing assessment in the classroom

Teachers today are seriously concerned at the inordinate amount of time likely to be taken up by assessment. The problems may not appear to be so serious in special schools, where classes are smaller and where there are likely to be two adults in each classroom. Nevertheless, it is essential to consider ways of improving practice and to recognize that the move from individual teaching to work with groups may have its effect on accurate assessment.

Recent research provides an example of managing assessment in a classroom of infants (Lacey, 1991). The PLAN/REVIEW model of working, described by teachers in the High Scope project in the USA (Hohmann *et al.*, 1983), is used by the teacher. She encourages the pupils to negotiate the tasks of the day, which are then carried out individually or, under her supervision, in small groups. Files or individual programmes are not written up during the session but children are encouraged to review their work. Each child uses a piece of work or a related object as a prompt and the teacher observes and records this review. Assessment is seen as an integral part of each session, but it is never allowed to interfere with the flow of work. Prompts, without being prescriptive, determine the nature of the classroom environment and are clear indicators of the children's achievements. They enable both the children and the teacher to reflect on what has been learned. Assessment is, in TGAT's terms, formative, as the teacher's observations will be used to determine future planning.

Pupil involvement

The involvement of pupils in their own assessment is essential, even for those with special learning difficulties. Galton (1989) suggests that assessment should be seen not so much as judgements on tasks completed but rather as a dialogue between teacher and pupil, during which standards are set and mutual criteria agreed. It then becomes part of a process which leads to an holistic view of negotiated learning in which pupils develop a clear understanding of the reasons for, and the nature of, their learning. Ainscow and Muncey (1989) stress the importance of this clarity, and suggest that 'whenever children are observed not getting on with their work, they usually lack a basic understanding of its purpose' (p. 84). If children are able to relate experiences directly to their existing knowledge, learning is much more likely to take place.

Negotiating with pupils is undoubtedly time-consuming but as developments in Records of Achievement have shown, it can be very effective. Pupils are helped to identify short-term educational and personal goals which are both challenging and achievable and the results are built into a profile to which they have contributed and which reflects their achievements in all areas. Records of Achievement should now be an integral part of every curriculum (Broadfoot, 1986).

The following account is taken from the West Midlands' Monitoring Group SLD's Broadsheet No.5: Assessment (1991) and shows how Records of Achievement can become part of a whole school's assessment policy:

> Circular 8/90 (DES, 1990b) Records of Achievement (ROAs) states that 'The Government see ROAs as integrally linked with the National Curriculum. The underlying principles of recognising positive achievement in all pupils are common to both. ROA schemes have often served to bring together schools' policies and practices on assessment, recording and reporting into a coherent whole. The Secretary of State applauds such developments, which are very much in the spirit of the National Curriculum' (p. 99).

Records of Achievement are already in place in many schools for pupils with Severe Learning Difficulties. They have been introduced, for example, in Sandwell as a requirement for TVE Extension, which embraces all schools and colleges with secondary-age pupils. ROAs have proved to be a valuable tool in assessing students with learning difficulties against a recognized set of criteria in areas such as Work Experience, Science and Creative Arts. They are also a vehicle for student self-assessment in areas such as Personal and Social Education, Physical Education and Games, Life Skills and outside school activities.

At the present time ROAs are generally only used with pupils during their final two years at school, but there is no reason why they cannot be used throughout a child's school life as a mean of integrating the various curriculum, communication and accountability aspects of assessment.

Integrated assessment would include:

the diagnostic;
pupil self-assessment;
periodic assessment;

all of which lead to a school-leaving certificate and form the basis for institutional review and evaluation.

A Record of Achievement entails both Formative and Summative Documents.

The Formative Document is an ongoing process which is integrated within the curriculum and

supports curriculum development;
involves the pupil in dialogue (in the appropriate mode);
is a frequent and continuous record;
is constructive;
emphasizes positive achievement.

The Summative Document is the final statement which

takes into account vocational/post-school needs;
gives a rounded portrayal;
emphasizes positive achievements;
uses a variety of sources of evidence/information.

The formative/summative processes can be recorded by using video recorders, cameras, word processors (with concept keyboard/ graphics), and tape recorders.

In order to use a Record of Achievement for subject attainment, clear objectives would need to be set and explained to the pupil.

The assessment itself would indicate how far individual pupils have achieved the set objectives by self- and teacher-assessment.

It would be essential to divide work into manageable units using National Curriculum Assessment targets, tied into the objectives/criteria already being used in the school. The school also needs to revise (or use existing) continuous assessment materials, and to consider their relationship to present/future record-keeping by teachers. Records of Achievement should not be used to reshape teaching programmes, but should be seen as an integral part of the total process.

Multi- and inter-disciplinary factors

During future developments in teacher assessment, consideration should be given to the role of inter-disciplinary assessment, which is already well established in some schools for pupils with severe learning difficulties. Assessment needs to be regarded as a joint enterprise, between pupils, parents, teachers and other professionals, to identify and understand the nature of a child's difficulties and needs. When teachers are free to work alongside other professionals and recognize and understand additional skills, they can begin to provide appropriate learning experiences for their pupils. Kellmer Pringle (1981) stresses the need for trust between professionals based on the acceptance of the fact that an isolated professional will never find the 'key' to the solution of a child's problems. Sutton (1981) develops the point and stresses that professionalism must never attempt to 'police and control' their own areas of specialism. The 'key' can only be found in inter-disciplinary cooperation.

School policy

All teachers, in any school, need to be fully involved at every stage in the development of a meaningful whole-school policy on curriculum and assessment. Unfortunately, the Department of Education and

Science's decision to create separate bodies – the National Curriculum Council to oversee and advise on the curriculum, and the Schools Examination and Assessment Council to take responsibility for assessment – has encouraged teachers to regard curriculum and assessment as distinct and unconnected areas. The use of a coordinator, responsible in a school for both the overall development of the curriculum and assessment, is a positive and progressive method of redressing the balance. It is imperative for assessment to be an integral part of the whole teaching and learning process, in which pupils are essential partners, and for documents to form a dynamic profile, available to all of the pupil's teachers, throughout his school life. Pupils will only reach their full potential when, through participation in their own education, they are encouraged to move towards responsibility and independence.

Note

The editor wishes to thank Steve Parker (Chairman) and members of the Assessment Working Party of the West Midlands Monitoring Group SLD (1991) for permission to use extracts from 'Records of Achievement' in Broadsheet – 5.

References

Ainscow, M. and Tweddle, D. (1979) *Preventing Classroom Failure. An Objectives Approach*. Chichester: John Wiley.

Ainscow, M. and Tweddle, D. (1984) *Early Learning Skills Analysis*. Chichester: John Wiley.

Ainscow, M. and Muncey, J. (1989) *Meeting Individual Needs*. London: David Fulton.

Barrs, M., Ellis, S., Hester, H. and Thomas, A. (1988) *The Primary Language Record*. London: ILEA.

Bayley, N. (1969) *Bayley Scales of Infant Development*. New York: Psychological Corporation.

Brennan, W.K. (1985) *Curriculum for Special Needs*. Milton Keynes: Open University Press.

Broadfoot, P. (1986) *Profiles and ROAs*. London: Holt, Rinehart & Winston.

Campione, J. (1989) 'Assisted Assessment: a taxonomy of approaches and an outline of strength and weaknesses', *American Journal of Learning Disabilities*, 22, 3, pp. 151–65.

Cooper, D. (1987) 'TVEI: Across the Ability Range?', *British Journal of Special Education*, 14, 4, pp. 13–15.

Coupe, J. and Porter, J. (Eds) (1986) *The Education of Children with Severe Learning Difficulties. Bridging the Gap Between Theory and Practice*. London: Croom Helm.

Crawford, N.B. (Ed.) (1980) *Curriculum Planning for the ESN(s) Child.* Kidderminister: BIMH.

Department of Education and Science (1978) *Special Educational Needs: Report of the Committee of Enquiry into the Education of Handicapped Children and Young People* (The Warnock Report). London: HMSO.

Department of Education and Science (1988) *National Curriculum Task Group on Assessment and Testing* (TGAT Report). London: HMSO.

Department of Education and Science (1988) *Education Reform Act 1988.* London: HMSO.

Department of Education and Science (1990a) *Education Observed: Special Needs Issues. A Survey by HMI.* London: HMSO.

Department of Education and Science (1990b) *Records of Achievement,* Circular 8/90. London: HMSO.

East Sussex SLD Schools (1990) *Is This English?* East Sussex SLD Schools. National Curriculum Guide.

East Sussex SLD Schools (1990) *Does it Add Up?* East Sussex SLD Schools. National Curriculum Guide.

East Sussex SLD Schools (1990) *We Can All Learn Science.* National Curriculum Guide.

Fagg, S., Aherne, P., Skelton, S. and Thornber, A. (1990) *Entitlement for All in Practice.* London: David Fulton.

Feuerstein, R., Rand, Y. and Hoffman, M. B. (1979) *The Dynamic Assessment of Retarded Performers.* Baltimore: University Park Press.

Galton, M. (1989) *Teaching in the Primary School.* London: David Fulton.

Gardner, J., Murphy, J. and Crawford, N. (1983) *The Skills Analysis Model.* Kidderminster: BIMH Publications.

Gipps, C. (1990) *Assessment: A Teachers' Guide to the Issues.* London: Hodder & Stoughton.

Glenn, S. (1988) 'Interactive approaches to working with children with profound and multiple learning difficulties', in Smith, B. (Ed.) *Interactive Approaches to the Education of Children with Severe Learning Difficulties.* Birmingham: Westhill College.

Goddard, A. (1983) 'Processes in special education', in Blenkin, G. and Kelly, A. V. (Eds) *The Primary Curriculum in Action. A Process Approach to Educational Practice.* London: Harper Row.

Gordon, P. and Lawton, D. (Eds) (1978) *Curriculum Change and the Nineteenth and Twentieth Centuries.* London: Hodder & Stoughton.

Griffiths, R. (1954) *The Abilities of Babies.* London: University of London Press.

Harris, J. (1990) *Early Language Development. Implications for Clinical and Educational Practice.* London: Routledge.

Hill, P. M. and Nicolich, L. M. (1981) 'Pretend play and patterns of cognition in Down's syndrome children', *Child Development,* 52, pp. 611–17.

Hohmann, M., Banet, B. and Weikart, D. P. (1979) *Young Children in Action.* Michigan: High/Scope Press.

Hughes, M. (1986) *Children and Number.* Oxford: Blackwell.

Hurt, J. (1988) *Outside the Mainstream. A History of Special Education.* London: Batsford.

74

Kellmer Pringle, M. (1981) 'Partnership in Practice', in NCSE (Ed.) *Partnership in Special Education. Report of the 9th National Conference of NCSE*. Southampton: NCSE.

Kerr, J. F. (Ed.) (1968) *Changing the Curriculum*. London: University of London Press.

Lacey, P. (1991) 'Strategies for Teachers'. Unpublished M. Ed. Dissertation, Birmingham University.

Laycock, E. (1990) 'The Process Project'. Unpublished Lecture.

Le Normand, M. T. (1986) 'A developmental exploration of language used to accompany symbolic play in young, normal children (2–4 years old)', *Child Care, Health and Development*, 12, pp. 121–34.

Leeming, K., Swann, W., Coupe, J. and Mittler, P. (1979) *Teaching Language and Communication to the Mentally Handicapped. Schools Council Bulletin 8*. London: Evans/Methuen.

Lowe, M. and Costello, A. J. (1973) *The Symbolic Play Test*. Windsor: NFER-Nelson.

McConkey, R. (1981) 'Education without understanding', *Special Education: Forward Trends*, 8, 3, pp. 8–10.

Mittler, P. (1979) *Teaching Children with Severe Learning Difficulties. Stanley Segal Lecture 1978*. Tunbridge Wells: Costello Educational.

National Curriculum Council (1990) *Curriculum Guidance 3: The Whole Curriculum*. York: NCC.

Nind, M. and Hewett, D. (1988) 'Interaction as curriculum', *British Journal of Special Education*, 15, 2, pp.55–7.

Ouvry, C. (1987) *Educating Children with Profound Handicaps*. Kidderminister: BIMH.

Reynell, J. K. (1977) *Reynell Developmental Language Scales: Revised*. Windsor: NFER-Nelson.

Smith, B. (Ed.) (1988) *Interactive Approaches to the Education of Children with Severe Learning Difficulties*. Birmingham: Westhill College.

Smith, B. (1989) 'Which approach?', *Mental Handicap*, 17, 3, pp. 111–15.

Smith, B., Moore, Y. and Phillips, C. J. (1983) 'Education with understanding?', *Special Education: Forward Trends*, 10, 2, pp. 21–4.

Staff of Tye Green School (1991) 'Broad, balanced and relevant?', *Special Children*, January, 44, pp. 11–13.

Sutton, A. (1981) 'The social role of the educational psychologist in the definition of educational subnormality', in Barton, L. and Tomlinson, S. (Eds) *Special Education Policy. Practices and Social Issues*. London: Harper & Row.

Tansley, A. E. and Gulliford, R. (1960) *The Education of Slow Learning Children*. London: Routledge & Kegan Paul.

Thorndike, R. L., Hagen, E. and Sattler, J. (1985) *Standford-Binet Intelligence Scale*. Chicago, Ill: The Riverside Publishing Company.

Ware, J. (1990) 'The National Curriculum for pupils with severe learning difficulties', in Daniels, H. and Ware, J. (Eds) *Special Educational Needs and the National Curriculum*. London: Kogan Page.

Watson, J. (1990) 'Language facilitation within the classroom', *British Journal of Special Education*, 17, 4, pp. 144–7.

Wechsler, D. (1974) *The Wechsler Intelligence Scale for Children – Revised*. New York: Psychological Corporation.

Wedell, K. (1990) 'Overview. The 1998 Act and current principles of special educational needs', in Daniels, H. and Ware, J. (Eds) *Special Educational Needs and the National Curriculum*. London: Kogan Page.

Wells, G. (1985) *Language Development in the Pre-School Years*. Cambridge: Cambridge University Press.

West Midlands Monitoring Group SLD (1989) Broadsheet No. 2. National Curriculum Monitoring Group (SLD) West Midlands.

West Midlands Monitoring Group SLD (1990) Broadsheet No. 3. National Curriculum Monitoring Group (SLD) West Midlands.

West Midlands Monitoring Group SLD (1991a) Broadsheet No. 4. National Curriculum Monitoring Group (SLD) West Midlands.

West Midlands Monitoring Group SLD (1991b) Broadsheet No. 5. National Curriculum Monitoring Group (SLD) West Midlands.

White, M. and Cameron, R. J. (1987) *The Portage Early Education Programme* (Revised UK Version). Windsor: NFER-Nelson.

Wilson, M. D. (1981) *The Curriculum in Special Schools*. London: Schools Council.

CHAPTER 6

Dual Disablement

Sudarshan Abrol, Christina Tilstone and Elizabeth Yates

Britain has been a multicultural society for over 2000 years (Farrell, 1990) and most immigrants have been absorbed into the education system with little attention given to their backgrounds and cultural identities. Since the increase in the numbers of Afro-Caribbean and Asian immigrants, there has been an over-representation of black children in special education (DES, 1974; OECD, 1987; Tomlinson, 1990). The situation has stemmed, in the main, from the policies of the 1960s when it was considered that immigrant children, especially those whose first language was not English had 'special needs' (Tomlinson, 1990).

Discussions on the most effective strategies for integration have often been inhibited by inaccurate (and contentious) terminology and it is essential to define some of the terms used in this chapter. They are taken or adapted from the relevant literature and are in accord with the values and perceptions of the authors:

- *Multicultural education*: educational provision which reflects the rich and diverse nature of Britain's multi-ethnic and multi-racial society.
- *Racism*: an ideology of racial domination and exploitation that incorporates belief in a particular race's cultural and/or inherent biological inferiority and uses them to justify and prescribe inferior or unequal treatment (Cohen and Manion, 1983).
- *Black*: a term used by the authors to indicate non-whites. It should be stressed that it is used throughout without any ideological, or other, implications or connotations.
- *Asian*: persons born in India, Pakistan or Bangladesh and the

descendants of such persons who were born in East Africa. It also includes their descendants born in the UK. The persons to whom the term is applied may not necessarily define themselves as Asians, or if they do, may not recognize it as a predominant self-identity (Baxter *et al.*, 1990)

- *Afro-Caribbean*: persons of African origin who were born in one of the Caribbean Islands and their descendants born in the UK (ibid.).

The placement of the children of immigrants in special schools was often the resource-led answer to problems, and many educationalists continue to maintain (either from ignorance or for convenience) 'that difficulties with English lead to poor educational performance and learning difficulties' (Tomlinson, 1990, p. 3). Little has been written about the dilemmas facing teachers in schools for pupils with severe learning difficulties with a high proportion of children from the families of black immigrants. This chapter is in essence a plea to teachers to document their work and to share their knowledge. There is some indication of creative and innovative practice in cities with large black populations (Birmingham, Coventry and Bradford) but it is rarely shared through the literature. Developments in home/school contacts, supportive learning programmes, and language learning, are backed up by strong LEA policy-initiatives which make appropriate attempts to meet current needs. It is the term 'appropriate to need' which is all important, as Baxter *et al.* (1990) emphasize:

> Many services for people with learning difficulties are undergoing reform, often on the basis of new philosophies geared towards change. But we need to exercise caution. The relevance of some of these concepts to the lives of many black and ethnic minority people in our society is not necessarily clear. With the best will in the world, black and ethnic minority people with learning difficulties could be further disadvantaged by 'progressive' developments which are inappropriate to their needs (p. 9).

It may be assumed that such hindering 'progressive developments' are those initiated by white professionals who are not always aware of the requirements or feelings of black people. Unfortunately the work of black and ethnic minority organizations is undervalued and is consequently rarely recognized by educational establishments.

In Joginder Phull's case (Chapter 2) the temple played a vital role in supporting the family. One school for pupils with severe learning difficulties in the Midlands encourages the religious leaders of both Afro-Caribbean and Asian communities to accompany out-reach workers on visits to the family, and to take an active part in curriculum delivery. Such practices are common in areas where there are large numbers of pupils from ethnic minorities, but may not be so widespread in schools containing smaller numbers.

It has been stated that black people with severe learning difficulties fall into two minority groups, that of ethnic minority and that of severe learning difficulties. Hicks (1981) emphasizes that most minority groups 'share several characteristics: particular physical and/or cultural traits; unequal treatment; and a perception of their separateness' (p. 6). Some writers therefore consider that these people suffer from double discrimination (Abrol, 1990; Baxter *et al.*, 1990; Williams, 1984). Double discrimination is not a consequence of small numbers, but results from a lack of social, political and economic power. Anti-racist and equal opportunities policies have done much to ensure parity but two extreme positions documented in the early 1980s are still evident in the provision of minority education (Churchill, 1983). At the end of the continuum is the firmly-held belief that minority groups will only be fully accepted into society after their language and culture is replaced by that of the majority. At the other end is the view that the minority language and culture must be preserved at all costs and should have the same social status as that of the majority. Nevertheless, 'multicultural pluralism' (which states that there should be equal opportunities, cultural diversity and mutual tolerance) has become generally accepted in education (Tomlinson, 1983). These opposing views must not be ignored by teachers of pupils with severe learning difficulties, for, although the teachers aim for independence in their pupils, they must consider the needs of black pupils with profound multiple learning difficulties who may become dependent solely on the care of relatives fluent only in their own mother tongue. Multicultural education, however, is not only concerned with teaching pupils from ethnic minorities, but also aims to prepare all pupils for life in a multicultural society.

Grugeon and Woods (1990) argue that each teacher's personal attributes are the major influences on the successful development of multicultural education. They list the essential qualities as commitment, a critical approach, creativity and curiosity; a list which could be applied to all aspects of special education! Willey (1982) also places emphasis on the attributes of the individual teacher:

> Nowhere is the role of the teacher more crucial than in the area of multicultural education, for its aims and objectives rely heavily for their effective implementation on the personal attitudes, skills and knowledge of the teacher (p. 30).

Unfortunately, many teachers are ill-equipped to take on this role, as multicultural education has had little or no place in their initial training. In 1983, Tomlinson stated that teacher training establishments were lacking in enthusiasm towards measures designed to prepare teachers for work in a multi-ethnic society. Student teachers at that time had very little knowledge of ethnic minority children and often displayed inappropriate attitudes. Very few were aware of the important role which they might be expected to play in society and, in short, were inadequately prepared.

The Swann Report (DES, 1985) subsequently recommended that all teachers should receive a compulsory component of multicultural education as part of their initial training. The Report also suggested that this should not be purely theoretical but that, if possible, students should have practical experience of working in schools in which there is cultural and racial diversity. These initiatives will help schools for pupils with severe learning difficulties in the future, provided, of course, that multicultural education also includes a 'special needs' focus. In-service education and training is so crucial in the development of multicultural perspectives that this chapter will consider the essential issues within the context of staff development for teachers and special school assistants.

Duncan (1986), in outlining a model for staff development in multicultural education, suggested there should be specific stages of INSET: investigation; learning; experimentation and adaptation. Gay, in Duncan (1986), develops the point and suggests the following framework:

(1) Basic information about ethnic and cultural pluralism.
(2) Knowledge acquisition and values clarification about ethnic groups and their cultures.
(3) Skill development in translating multicultural knowledge into programmes, practices, habits and behaviours of classroom instruction.
(4) Competence in making educational objectives, curriculum content and learning activities meaningful to the experiential backgrounds and frames of reference of all students (p. 147).

The authors consider that the second recommendation should be the starting point for discussion as it provides an important foundation on which to base future action.

Knowledge acquisition and values clarification

It is important for the staff of a school as a whole to discuss the standards and principles on which their curriculum is based. The essential question is, does the ethos of the school simply reflect the values of the white majority at the expense of the black minority? For example, Baxter *et al*. (1990) challenge the indiscriminate application of the principles of normalization (Wolfensberger, 1972). Although they see these as being based on the belief that people with learning difficulties must be allowed to lead lives which are as 'normal' or as 'valued' as possible, 'normalisation itself makes certain blanket assumptions about what is normal and valued in our society' (p. 13). They suggest that before these ideas can be implemented two key questions must be answered.

(1)   What are the norms our society takes for granted?
(2)   What values determine policy and practice?

It is therefore necessary to consider the values placed on those curriculum areas concerned with personal and social education (including sex education); social and self-help skills; leisure activities; English (including language and communication); as well as dress, appearance and behaviour. The authors give an example of a simple exercise carried out by the Harlesden Community Mental Handicap Team which highlighted the different values attached to such aspects as living independently and relationships with the opposite sex by white professionals and people from Afro-Caribbean and Asian communities. Statements which reflected concepts central to normalization (having a boyfriend/girlfriend; going to a pub/disco; being extrovert) were valued by white professionals but were unacceptable to people from black and ethnic minorities. There were also significant differences between the responses by Afro-Caribbeans and Asians.

Such discussions and debates not only help staff to view society from the position of minority communities, but also allow them to identify and to confront racism. Jeffcoate (1984) challenges the allegation that racism is practised by teachers and suggests that limited curriculum content is often the result of ignorance or 'curriculum inertia' on the part of teachers, rather than antagonism or a belief in the inferiority of the minority culture. The Swann Report, too, was critical of apathy and made reference to institutional racism, which it saw

> as describing the way in which a range of long established systems, practices and procedures, both within education and the wider society which were originally conceived and devised to meet the needs and aspirations of a relatively homogeneous society, can now be seen not only to fail to take account of the multicultural nature of Britain today

but may also ignore or even actively work against the interests of ethnic minority communities (DES, 1985, p. 28).

Many LEAs run Racism Awareness courses although some writers have reservations about their value (Sivanandan, 1985). However, Abbott *et al.* (1989) give a graphic account of how a three-day course went some way towards bringing about changes in schools. The authors see a combination of school-based initiatives and support from committed LEAs as providing the best conditions for progress.

Ethnic and cultural pluralism

Teachers need a range of information about the pupils themselves and about their cultural traditions and life-styles. Care must be taken that such information does not produce cultural stereotyping and labelling on the one hand, or a 'tokenism' curriculum on the other. Issues of gender and religion and, in some cases, class must be explored from an individual perspective if sweeping statements are to be avoided. Suggesting that all Asians use their fingers to eat with is as misleading as suggesting that all pupils with Down's syndrome are musical! A realistic programme of integration will need to take into account the essential differences between individuals, whether they are Muslims, Sikhs, Hindus or from any other minority group.

Teachers also need to obtain information on cultural traditions. The usual starting point is to be well-informed on religious festivals, music and dress. This approach has often been criticized as tokenism resulting in 'the steel band, sari and samosa experience' but such criticism tends to undervalue genuine attempts to understand cultural traditions. Farrell (1990) also takes this view and sees such 'tokenistic' initiatives as small steps in stages of development. He suggests INSET activities that will encourage teachers to progress and develop. Although his approaches are aimed at teachers in mainstream schools they are, with some adaptations, applicable to those teaching in schools for pupils with severe learning difficulties.

Programmes, practices and behaviour

The recommendations of the Swann Committee (DES, 1985) were concerned with education for all and ways in which it was to be achieved. The Report not only focused on the education of pupils from ethnic minorities, but stressed the importance of educating all children to take their place in a multi-racial society. 'All' includes pupils with severe learning difficulties and teachers have a duty to give every youngster, whatever his potential, the knowledge, understanding and skills to function 'as a citizen of the wider national society in which he lives and in the interdependent world community of which he is also a member' (p. 319). Fine words if you have profound multiple learning difficulties and are learning to interact with your immediate environment – or are they? Multicultural education should be a process which permeates the curriculum, not an appendage. The starting point must be the development of the interpersonal skills of tolerance, cooperation, friendship and respect for others. At the same time, curriculum content should be scrutinized to ensure that it reflects a multicultural frame of reference.

Farrell (1990) gives examples of the multicultural content for both theme and subject areas including those of the National Curriculum which all teachers of pupils with severe learning difficulties will find useful. If the specific educational needs of pupils from ethnic minorities are to be met, staff, must be aware of the three issues which present the greatest challenges: assessment, the involvement of parents in education, and language teaching (Tomlinson, 1990).

Assessment

There are two distinct forms of assessment. One may lead to statementing; the other is a teacher's own continuous monitoring of her pupils within the classroom. Assessment which might lead to statementing, based on white middle-class life styles and experiences, is being questioned as an acceptable basis for psychological testing. The use of pictures or objects which are totally unfamiliar to children from ethnic minority groups or materials which are offensive in some way are under close scrutiny:

> 'In our religion the pig and the dog are not really nice animals', says a Muslim health visitor. 'We find it very offensive when our children are tested on their ability to recognise a pink plastic pig. It is even worse when they are expected to respond positively to pigs and dogs. It's against our religion' (Ward et al., 1990, p. 21).

The problems of assessments carried out by white professionals who may not understand the cultural intricacies of the minority group have been well documented (Tomlinson, 1989; Grugeon and Woods, 1990). The latter authors give a graphic account of the process of statementing of an Asian pupil and the involvement of an Asian family, recounted by a white teacher friend. The following extracts illustrate a lack of understanding of cultural differences on the part of the psychologist. He had suggested

> that Mrs. Singh could help to improve Jeetinder's spoken and written language by reading to him at bedtime, and could help to improve his numeracy by encouraging him to spend and account for his pocket money. Both ideas were culturally alien to Mrs Singh. There were no English children's books in the house, and the boys did not shop on their own nor have regular pocket money (p. 62).

Teachers also need to examine curriculum materials and resources in schools and will find it a useful INSET exercise to devise criteria for their selection. This is also an effective method of challenging assumptions and values.

Parental involvement

The involvement of parents in their children's education has only been actively encouraged during recent years. It is now recognized that parents are the chief advocates for their children, that they are major influences on their development and that they have rights and responsibilities. The participation of parents from ethnic minorities in their children's education, however, has been more limited and, although not actively discouraged, it has, at times, been difficult to promote, particularly when the parents' first language is not English. As Tomlinson (1983) observes:

> It is noteworthy that several Asian academics have undertaken research into Asian children's educational performance, and all have stressed gaining more parental support for education, and improved home/school liaison and the value of home and school making a positive effort to understand one another (p. 59).

Communication problems may result in many parents becoming alienated from the professionals involved in their child's education. Unfortunately, the professionals themselves often interpret this inability to understand the complexities of the system as a lack of interest and individual needs tend to be overlooked. The provision of information in the relevant language, and the support of home/school liaison workers is helping to improve the situation. Parents need to understand the education system and to relate to the vast numbers of professionals involved with their child (speech therapists and physiotherapists, educational psychologists and others). They also need to feel confident and able to make valid and real contributions to the education of their children.

Few professionals involved in special education have a command of a range of minority languages. The solution to this specific problem may well lie with the education system itself: greater opportunities and more encouragement in schools, colleges and the universities for students from minority groups to enter the relevant professions, and Local Education Authorities could develop staffing policies which would reflect these initiatives.

The head of one Midlands school, realizing the difficulties many parents from black and ethnic minorities were having in entering into any sort of partnership with the school, persuaded the Authority (through leisure and community services) to fund a teacher to give English lessons to parents. Transport was arranged for them and issues such as door-to-door collection were sensitively handled. Women drivers or escorts collected the Asian mothers from their homes and the starting time of the sessions was flexible. All meetings were fully subscribed and the home/school liaison teacher attended in order to provide and receive information on the children. This initiative has helped to overcome the reticence of some parents whose first language is not English to enter the school building. Despite their concern that their children should do well, and their anxiety to hear how their children were progressing, many had found it either intimidating or impracticable to visit the school regularly. In this case the school was offering a service which was highly valued for its own sake, and went further in influencing partnerships in education than the usual provision of dress-making and cookery classes.

The appointment of a home/school liaison teacher who is bilingual is also a positive step towards encouraging contact and communication between home and school. It is important, however, to define the role and the aims clearly in order to avoid the duplication of social and educational welfare (Finch, Fry and Anderson, 1980, cited in Tomlinson, 1984). Tomlinson warns that these professionals may provide another 'layer' who may 'distance minority parents still further from their children's class teacher – the person they may actually want to see' (Tomlinson, 1984, p. 90). On the other hand, home/school liaison teachers can provide a valuable service in disseminating information but unfortunately they are seen as a luxury by many Authorities, and those who do see them as necessary are fighting to retain this service in the face of serious educational cuts.

Language teaching

Despite the problems experienced when pupils with severe learning difficulties attempt to acquire a second language and fluency in a new culture, little research has been carried out. Which language should be taught? Can he ever become fluent in two languages? How should he be taught? are common questions. The trend in all sectors of education has been to focus on 'mother-tongue support' (aiding minority language speakers) in the transition towards English. This work needs to be part of everyday class activities. Precise observation of cultural differences in pre-verbal communication and of the acquisition of the mother tongue in bilingual environments needs to be documented and disseminated. The information that is available appears to indicate that innovative work is being undertaken, but that it is not being closely monitored or evaluated.

The National Curriculum Council (1991) Circular No. 11 stresses that if schools are to meet the needs of bilingual pupils they must consider:

- how to ensure full access to the National Curriculum and assessment for all pupils;
- the value placed on languages other than English spoken by pupils and used in the classroom (p. 4).

Section 11 funding (administered by the Home Office) was more readily available in previous years and was sometimes abused by special schools. Teachers employed to help pupils overcome linguistic barriers found themselves 'filling in' for absent staff or asked to take on teaching which was not directly concerned with the linguistic needs of pupils from ethnic minorities. New funding arrangements can only be made to LEAs on the basis that grants will be used to assist pupils directly to gain full access to, and benefit from, mainstream services by removing linguistic and cultural barriers.

Curriculum content and learning activities

A curriculum, in any context, should cater for the needs of individuals and must reflect the different cultures and life-styles of all pupils. In planning a curriculum for pupils with severe learning difficulties from ethnic minorities, teachers should be aware of specific cultural factors, although it should be emphasized that it is important to avoid generalizations and consequent 'cultural stereotyping'. In some cases, skills which appear to be appropriate in school may be irrelevant or completely unacceptable at home within the family. Teachers, therefore, need to develop a curriculum which is meaningful to the pupils and which combines their own education knowledge with the expectations and circumstances of the parents in order to make education as effective as possible. The teaching of inappropriate skills and behaviours can be counter-productive and can lead to unnecessary tensions. There is a danger that the school may be perceived as undervaluing or misunderstanding the culture of a specific group. Striking examples are the difference in some Asian's attitudes to washing and dressing and feeding. Many 'prefer to take a shower rather than a bath, even if this means using a bucket of warm water and a jug in the absence of a shower unit as a bath is considered un-hygienic' (Abrol, 1990). As may Asian families (particularly Muslims) have retained traditional attitudes to dress, teachers need to be sensitive to stronly-held beliefs. Bare legs are often regarded as inde-cent and consequently Asian girls wear salwars and kameezs (trousers and tunics). Similarly, 'the use of cosmetics by unmarried girls is considered unacceptable, yet many schools encourage their use in beauty lessons' (Abrol, 1990).

Some teachers undoubedtly react adversely to their Asian pupils' eating habits and eating with fingers may be actively discouraged. A child, therefore, may be expected to reject the customs of his home as he crosses the school threshold for he has been taught at home to eat chapati and dal without using cutlery. The problem may appear minor, and almost insignificant, but a pupil with severe learning difficulties is unlikely to cope in a situation where two contrasting and conflicting skills are demanded. Full and serious consideration needs to be given to ways in which the curriculum can accommodate these differences.

Fluency in social interactions is essential, but raises the question of what to include in the curriculum. Here familiarity with the expectations of both cultures is important and all pupils in a class could experiment with a rich and mixed range of social rituals and greetings.

Mannerisms may pose a more difficult problem. An Asian pupil, when addressed by an adult, may have been taught not to look the adult in the face, whereas pupils from a European background are encouraged to do so. Successes in these areas of the curriculum will depend on imaginative teaching and on staff sensitive to the customs of all cultures. Value judgements are inadmissible. It has been argued that dual teaching, in this and other areas, can retard the progress of a pupil with severe learning difficulties. But this is education for life and for a community which must value the beliefs and customs of two cultures; a pupil who is only half-equipped is ill-equipped to take his place in, and make his contribution to, any society.

An essential element in the move towards independence for children of all ages, all backgrounds and all abilities is personal and social development. This has been defined in a variety of ways, but it is generally agreed that increased self-esteem, enhanced self-image and self-awareness are essential goals. Similarly, the acquisition of inter-personal skills and a basic knowledge of health and sex education must be priorities. Patterns of behaviour in these fundamental areas tend to be different in Asian cultures. The Asian family may be (as in the case of Joginder Phull) an extended family which can include grandparents, uncles, aunts, cousins, nephews, nieces and of course, brothers and sisters, all playing a direct role in the whole education of the child. Asian couples may wish to retain full responsibility for their children beyond marriage, and in turn children throughout their lives may accept responsibility for their parents and other members of the family. Asian children may benefit from the secure and warm environment provided by the large family unit, but there is no overt patting, kissing or hugging. Fathers tend not to touch their daughters from an early age; part of a cultural tradition and now an established custom. It is essential to ensure that the curriculum takes into account these differences and that an awareness of 'not worse (or better) but different' becomes part of the ethos of the school.

The importance of staff development cannot be overstated and training programmes must include opportunities for teachers to exchange ideas and to disseminate information. Then, and only then, will schools be able to ensure that *all* pupils are being prepared for life in the society of the future.

Note

The Editor wishes to thank Sudarshan Abrol and the publishers of *Special Children* for permission to use information from 'Curriculum and Culture', February 1990, in this chapter.

88

References

Abbott, B., Gilbert, S., Lawson, R., Burt, C. and Woods, P. 1989) 'Towards anti-racist awareness: confessions of some teacher converts', in Woods, P. (Ed.) *Working for Teacher Development*. Norfolk: Peter Francis.

Abrol, S. (1990) 'Curriculum and Culture', *Special Children*, Feb, 36, pp. 8–10.

Baxter, C., Poonia, K., Ward, L. and Nadirshaw, Z. (1990) *Double Discrimination. Issues and Services for People with Learning Difficulties from Black and Ethnic Minority Communities*. London: Kings Fund.

Churchill, S. (1983) *Problems and Policy Instruments in the Provision of Speical Education in OECD. The Education of Minority Groups. An Enquiry into Problems and Practices of Fifteen Countries*. Aldershot: Gower.

Cohen, L. and Manion, L. (1983) *Multi-cultural Classrooms*. London: Croom Helm.

Department of Education and Science (1974) *Educational Needs of Immigrants*. London: HMSO.

Department of Education and Science (1985) *Education for All. The Report of the Committee of Enquiry into the Education of Children from Ethnic Minority Groups* (The Swann Report). London: HMSO.

Duncan, C. (1986) 'Developing a multi-cultural approach to the curriculum', in Aurora, R. and Duncan, C. (Eds) *Multi-cultural Education: Towards Good Practice*. London: Routledge and Kegan Paul.

Farrell, P. (1990) *Multicultural Education*. Leamington Spa: Scholastic Publications.

Grugeon, E. and Woods, P. (1990) *Educating All. Multicultural Perspectives in the Primary School*. London: Routledge.

Hicks, D.W. (1981) *Minorities. A Teacher's Resource Book for the Multi-ethnic Curriculum*. London: Heinemann.

Jeffcoat, R. (1984) *Ethnic Minorities and Education*. London: Harper Row.

National Curriculum Council (1991) *Circular No. 11: Linguistic Diversity and the National Curriculum*. York: NCC.

Organisation for Economic Cooperation and Development (1987) *Immigrants' Children at School*. Paris: Centre for Educational Research and Innovation.

Sivanandan, A. (1985) 'RAT and the degradation of black struggle', *Race and Class*, XXVI, 4, pp. 1–33.

Tomlinson, S. (1983) *Ethnic Minorities in British Schools*. London: Heinemann Educational Books.

Tomlinson, S. (1984) *Home and School in Multicultural Britain*. London: Batsford.

Tomlinson, S. (1989) 'Asian pupils and special issues', *British Journal of Special Education*, 16, 3, pp. 119–22.

Tomlinson, S. (1990) 'Asian children with special needs – a broad perspective', in Orton, C. (Ed.) *Asian Children and Special Needs. A Report*. London: ACE.

Ward, L., Baxter, C., Poonia, K. and Nadirshaw, Z. (1990) 'An umbrella for the sun?', *Community Care*, 6 December, pp. 21–3.

89

Willey, R. (1982) *Teaching in Multicultural Britain*. York: Longman/Schools Concil.
Williams, Philip (Ed.) (1984) *Special Education in Minority Communities*. Milton Keynes: Open University Press.
Wolfensberger, W. (1972) *The Principle of Normalisation in Human Services*. Toronto: National Institute of Mental Retardation.

CHAPTER 7

Managing the Classroom Environment

Penny Lacey

Although its importance is often overlooked, the organization of the classroom environment plays a central role in teaching and learning within schools for children with severe learning difficulties. Too often rooms and corridors are cluttered with equipment and the ubiquitous music fills the air! Pupils are rushed past attractive displays with no chance to browse, and boxes of books lie hidden away in cupboards. An extreme view. Sadly, it still happens in some special schools.

Undoubtedly the environment reflects the beliefs and values of those who work within it. If a teacher believes in the importance of encouraging independence in pupils, the classroom will be arranged to allow open access to all resources. Shelves will be labelled with words or symbols to encourage pupils to fetch and return essential equipment; books will be easily accessible; staff will encourage pupils to think for themselves and to help each other (Hohmann *et al.*, 1979).

There are, however, many pupils with severe learning difficulties who do not fit easily into situations designed for this style of teaching and learning. Independent responses are not always acceptable from pupils with challenging behaviours or with profound and multiple learning difficulties and the approaches used by classroom staff are reflected in the classroom environment. Pupils with profound and multiple learning difficulties may need conditions which are relatively unstimulating in order that they can concentrate effectively on specific stimuli (Evans and Ware, 1987). Access to a limited number of resources at any one time may be necessary for pupils with challenging

90

behaviours, but the widely differing individual needs found in any classroom must be taken into account. Consequently, staff may face considerable problems when organizing the environment.

Organizational structure does not necessarily lead to rigidity, and if 'the classroom' is extended to include all corners of the school, new and unexpected environments can be created to meet diverse needs. Many schools no longer have 'Special Care' classes and consequently pupils with profound and complex learning difficulties are integrated throughout the school. If teachers are to respond to their needs, it may become necessary to time-table specific resource areas for their use. Some schools use 'dark' or 'white' rooms in which stimuli can be carefully controlled; others have areas reserved for motor work. Special storage areas have been created in some cases, where all the bulky equipment designed to encourage sitting, standing and walking can be stored and is easily accessible. Classrooms, too, can be arranged in a variety of ways to provide sensory areas. Longhorn (1988) gives classroom plans which include areas for specific sensory stimuli. Problems, however, can arise. Specialized areas can be difficult to maintain if pupils exhibit disruptive behaviours.

In Chapter 5 of this book, some attention is given to the variety of teaching approaches found in schools for children with severe learning difficulties. These methods fall into two areas: individual direct instruction and group learning. The former has largely been influenced by behaviourist theory; the latter by cognitive views of learning. As many teachers make good use of both methods and see them as complementary, classroom layouts need to be adaptable.

Earlier developments in the teaching of pupils with severe learning difficulties tended to concentrate on individual instruction to the exclusion of other approaches. The cross-curricular elements underpinning National Curriculum documents, however, demand collaboration, and recent research in primary education stresses the importance of pupils working in groups (Bennett, 1989). Bruner's view of learning through social interaction also supports the notion of group problem-solving (Wood, 1988). The organization of group work with pupils with severe learning difficulties is demanding and requires more careful planning than in mainstream classes (Rose, 1991). Pupils may need encouragement to interact and it is often necessary to focus intitially on learning to work with a partner, who might be an adult or a more-able person. The work of Veronica Sherborne (1990) in physical education emphasizes the value of working together and building relationships.

It is evident that there may be a wide variety of abilities and needs in any one class of pupils with severe learning difficulties, but as heterogeneous groups often function better (Dunne and Bennett, 1990) teachers can make effective use of these differences. At a basic level, pupils could collaborate to produce a collage: one selecting materials, another cutting them up, a third pasting and a fourth arranging. Collaboration would be encouraged if the whole picture were to be discussed while it was being created. Individual needs can be catered for by the selection of tasks and by the assistance offered, whether by adults or other members of the group.

Although classes in special schools are small, it may be necessary for teachers to work with sub-groups or with individual pupils. The implications are that other pupils may need to work independently, possibly on undemanding tasks (sometimes referred to as 'holding activities') which are often inappropriate. Teachers in primary schools have devised more demanding organizational models and one school identified three levels of learning tasks. The first is teacher-intensive and involves new learning; the second requires the teacher to introduce the task and then withdraw; the third engages pupils in the solution of their own problems without help from a teacher, but relying on support from other members of the group in order to produce a joint piece of work. The National Curriculum Council (1990) video and workbook *Working Together* gives examples of this kind of collaboration at Key Stages 1 and 2.

Formerly it was not usually possible for pupils with severe learning difficulties to work together in this way as individual programmes and the practising of isolated skills out of context were customary. It may still be necessary, however, to focus on a particular skill to ensure that progress is being made. This should be done in the appropriate context in order to enable pupils to respond to the wider environment.

Controlling the environment is a key to working with pupils with severe learning difficulties. This does not, however, imply that all control is necessarily in the hands of the teacher. Consultation with pupils who are able to respond can be an extremely useful learning opportunity. Mainstream pupils in the early years can negotiate complex rules for classroom organization including the acceptance of the need for teachers to have some uninterrupted time with individuals or small groups (Galton, 1989). Older pupils with severe learning difficulties could also be involved in discussions on the specific physical environment that they would favour and on the rules necessary for the smooth running of the classroom. Ultimately, however, staff must ensure that negotiations reflect the needs of all pupils in the class, including those with profound and multiple learning difficulties.

Although the skills required for problem-solving and generalization are not easily acquired by many pupils with severe learning difficulties, it is possible to devise strategies to encourage the making of connections. A useful example is of a child learning to cross the road. First, the adult holds his hand and they cross together; second, the adult continues to hold his hand but 'talks' him through the situation; later he crosses alongside the adult who provides a running commentary on the required actions. At the next stage the process is determined by careful questioning, starting with 'What do we do first?' Finally the child is allowed to take the lead and direct the adult. Only then is he allowed to cross alone. This model, with its emphasis on pupil responsibility, can be used to encourage and develop self-regulatory behaviours in a variety of contexts.

It is difficult to foster decision-making and problem-solving if pupils are not offered choices. Teaching and learning influenced solely by behavioural theory features 'errorless learning', but 'learning through mistakes' in a positive, accepting and secure environment can be highly effective. One quickly learns the importance of remembering to take a towel to the swimming baths when the consequences of forgetting (feeling wet and cold and miserable) are experienced. Teachers are often too eager to help pupils to avoid such mistakes, and eliminate the opportunities offered. Negotiations to share or borrow a friend's towel and other chances to encourage self-regulation or to reduce dependence on adults are invaluable. Teachers should devise similar, relevant strategies for other contexts.

Work of this kind has been developed by the Staff of Rectory Paddock School (1983), including the strategies of verbal rehearsal, imagery elaboration, and executive control (self-monitoring). Metacognition (or learning how to learn) is seen as an important part of the curriculum and pupils are encouraged to think for themselves in problem-solving situations with sensitive teacher intervention. An interesting example of an executive-control, tasks-record sheet illustrates the principle of looking at a problem, suggesting a strategy, trying it out, and evaluating it with the aid of an adult who provides helpful prompts and support. The written curriculum of the school includes a variety of games and activities which help pupils to develop a greater ability to 'learn how to learn'. Taking messages, fetching items from a list and 'Kim's game' are effective, but it is also necessary to create an atmosphere which promotes problem-solving behaviours.

Often, teachers may need to 'sabotage' the environment in order to create problems for pupils to solve: too few chairs, the wrong kind of drink in a jug, coats jumbled up, a lack of tables, and a stranger in the classroom who needs help. Judicious questions and prompts can produce excellent learning situations and effective motivation.

Questioning is a very important part of a problem-solving environment for pupils with severe learning difficulties and it can present useful challenges. Teacher questioning, however, can be counter-productive if lower-order questions (which focus on the learning of facts or require only 'yes' or 'no' answers) are used. More thoughtful responses, which demonstrate the handling and processing of ideas, need to be encouraged (Kerry, 1982; Perrott, 1982). Helping pupils with severe learning difficulties to answer these higher-order questions is difficult but not impossible. When working alongside children, teachers can provide appropriate models of questioning which can subsequently be used by the pupils themselves. Science and technology activities lend themselves to this mode of working but the strategies can be used effectively in all other areas of the curriculum.

The approach is known as 'scaffolding' upon which pupils can build their own understanding and skills. The work of various researchers into learning in nursery schools suggests that young children need direct support from adults if they are to begin to develop their own abilities as effective problem-solvers (Meadows and Cashdan, 1988; Tizard and Hughes, 1984). Children do not respond effectively when they are constantly 'told what to do' or if they are continually faced with unstructured environments. A guiding adult is essential to help the child to plan, to carry out activities and to reflect upon the outcome.

The High/Scope programme of pre-school education has much to offer to a problem-solving or cognitively-orientated environment. High/Scope, which originated in Michigan in the USA, combines the theory of active learning with that of daily planning by the children themselves. After assessment, staff plan appropriate experiences to help children to assume responsibilities, to take initiatives, to be creative, to make plans and to solve problems. Children are encouraged to use the sequence of PLAN–DO–REVIEW which offers a structure to both teachers and pupils as they work in the classroom.

> In the High/Scope classroom, children are encouraged to help make deliberate choices about their activities, to carry out their own plans, and then to discuss the outcome with adults and peers (Langdown, 1989, p. 9).

All pupils with severe learning difficulties can benefit from this sequence and even those with limited oral skills can be encouraged to make choices and to look back on what they have achieved. Objects, photographs, signs or symbols can be used to help in this reflective process as teachers provide some of the 'scaffolding' needed by all learners in order to build new learning on the old (Wood, 1988).

Teachers in schools for pupils with severe learning difficulties who used the principles of High/Scope report that children are making more decisions for themselves, becoming less reliant on adults and developing appropriate independence skills more quickly, but objective evaluation is not yet available. The review sessions are particularly productive and even young children with severe learning difficulties can become involved in simple evaluation by showing their completed work. Although the High/Scope material is aimed specifically at pre-school education, the principles upon which it is based are central to all learning. Although the planning and evaluation of activities and experiences have rarely been fully exploited in work with pupils with profound and multiple learning difficulties, both contribute to the 'learning how to learn' elements in a 'broad and balanced curriculum'.

A High/Scope environment requires careful organization of the available space. For young children, it is helpful to provide separate work areas with distinctive equipment in order that clear choices can be made. For older pupils with severe learning difficulties, areas could be set aside for vocational, domestic and conventional academic work. The establishment of a daily routine within this physical environment is important if the sequence of planning, doing and reviewing is to become part of the learner's way of life (Hohmann et al., 1979).

The creation of an effective learning environment, however, involves more than a consideration of the physical surroundings. The focus is upon pupils and adults working together in situations where opportunities for negotiation are encouraged. Teachers of pupils with profound and multiple learning difficulties need to be skilled at interpreting non-verbal signals in order to enable each member of the group to make positive and meaningful contributions to work in progress. It should always be borne in mind that every pupil has a right to influence his own learning. Pupil profiling and Records of Achievement reflect these working methods especially as they influence the developing curriculum (see Chapters 3 and 5).

The management of an environment which encourages effective learning presents a challenge and compromises will have to be made in order to accommodate the different learning styles of individuals (Pollard and Tann, 1987), their specific needs and the demands of the curriculum. The wider management challenge of the multi-disciplinary team is considered in detail in Chapter 8, but it is also useful to examine ways in which teachers and special support assistants can together make the most effective use of the learning environment. It must be recognized, however that individual beliefs and values need to be explored and common goals agreed in order that the strengths of individuals are utilized and that equal partnership does not lead to a loss of individuality but ensures that all are fully involved (Knight, and Bowers, 1984).

Sturmey and Crisp (1986) discuss the possibility of utilizing the research strategy of 'Room Management' in day-to-day teaching and learning. Briefly, this requires three adults in the classroom, each of whom takes on a specific role. The 'individual helper' teaches individuals or groups of pupils; the 'activity manager' ensures that the rest of the pupils are kept on task; the 'mover' is responsible for resources and deals with interruptions. As the roles are separate and distinct, the model ensures that one adult is freed from routine matters and is able to concentrate fully on teaching. The model could, in some circumstances, combine the roles of 'activity manager' and 'mover' or possibly transfer some of the responsibilities of the 'mover' to selected pupils, who would then enter into full negotiation and collaboration with the adults involved.

The teacher is also responsible for the management of resources and for the most efficient use of space to meet the needs of pupils. There are many recent examples of imaginative ways in which environments can be designed to stimulate learning. In one, interest in the importance of literacy beyond the usual social sight-vocabulary for pupils with severe learning difficulties led to the creation of a comfortable, exciting and stimulating literacy area, containing a variety of reading materials; provision for writing (including such stimuli as familiar photographs, illustrations and tape recordings); resources for the making of the pupils' own books; and micro-processors (Ackerman and Mount, in press). In another school, 'dual language' books were produced in which symbols and simplified texts had been added to commercially-produced materials. A third school focused on creative writing, with a teacher acting as 'scribe' in order to avoid the inhibition of creative ideas as a result of physical difficulties in writing. The results were well-written stories, far exceeding the expectations of the teacher involved (Drinkwater, 1990).

The use of symbols in a literacy environment for pupils with severe learning difficulties makes possible a multi-modal approach to language acquisition. Symbols are particularly useful as a bridge between pictorial representation and the words themselves and they can be used in books, on displays, on labels for resources, on captions for photographs and illustrations, and on the timetable (Carpenter, in press).

The creation of an atmosphere in which effective learning can take place is the responsibility of all staff and should be reflected in whole-school policies. Staff need to provide experiences, activities, opportunities for interactions and sensory stimulation which, when carefully managed, can enable effective learning to take place. Arbitrary and random stimuli are rarely productive and careful selection is essential for meaningful development.

References

Ackerman, D. and Mount, H. (in press) *Literacy for All*. London: David Fulton.

Bennett, N. (1989) 'Classroom-based assessment. The National Curriculum and beyond', in Alexander, R. (Ed.) *Assessment in the Primary Classroom*. Bristol: Bristol Polytechnic.

Carpenter, B. (in press) 'Unlocking access to English in the National Curriculum', in Smith, B. (Ed.) *Interactive Approaches to the Core Subjects*. Bristol: Lame Duck Press.

Drinkwater, L. (1990) Unpublished B.Ed. project on Creative Writing. Birmingham: Westhill College.

Dunne, E. and Bennett, N. (1990) *Talking and Learning in Groups*. London: Macmillan.

Evans, P. and Ware, J. (1987) *'Special Care' Provision: The Education of Children with Profound and Multiple Learning Difficulties*. Windsor: NFER-Nelson.

Galton, M. (1989) *Teaching in the Primary School*. London: David Fulton.

Hohmann, M., Banet, B. and Weikart, D. (1979) *Young Children in Action*. Michigan: High/Scope Press.

Kerry, T. (1982) *Effective Questioning*. London: Macmillan.

Knight, R. and Bowers, T. (1984) 'Developing effective teams', in Bowers, T. (Ed.) *Management and the Special School*. London: Croom Helm.

Langdown, A. (1989) *Getting Started*. London: VOLCUF.

Longhorn, F. (1988) *A Sensory Curriculum for Very Special People*. London: Souvenir Press.

Meadows, S. and Cashdan, A. (1988) *Helping Children Learn*. London: David Fulton.

National Curriculum Council (1990) *Working Together*. York: NCC.

Perrott, E. (1982) *Effective Teaching*. London: Longman.

98

Pollard, A. and Tann, S. (1987) *Reflective Teaching in the Primary School*. London: Cassell.

Rose, R. (1991) 'A jigsaw approach to groupwork', *British Journal of Special Education*, 18, 2, pp. 54–8.

Sherborne, V. (1990) *Developmental Movement for Children*. Cambridge: Cambridge University Press.

Staff of Rectory Paddock School (1983) *In Search of a Curriculum*. Kent: Robin Wren.

Sturmey, P. and Crisp, T. (1986) 'Classroom management', in Coupe, J. and Porter, J. (Eds) *The Education of Children with Severe Learning Difficulties: Bridging the Gap Between Theory and Practice*. London: Croom Helm.

Tizard, B. and Hughes, M. (1984) *Young Children Learning*. London: Fontana.

Wood, D. (1988) *How Children Think and Learn*. Oxford: Blackwell.

CHAPTER 8

Working Collaboratively within a Multi-disciplinary Framework

Frank Steel

> The one important aspect about a Special School is that within its walls works a multi-disciplinary team of personnel and each member of the team . . . is dependent upon each other to enable each pupil to gain fully from this special experience (Burnham and Brayton, 1988, p. 7).

By their very nature, special schools provide the context within which professionals from different disciplines can work closely together for the benefit of pupils with a wide range of special needs. Thomson (1984) makes the point that 'the ethos of special education is one which sees everything which concerns the child's growth to maturity as coming within its grasp' (p. 120) and it is this holistic view which establishes the rationale for cooperation between disparate disciplines.

The 'medical' or 'deficit' model of assessment which categorized children according to their disabilities or limitations and consequently imposed an artificial barrier between 'treatment' and 'education' has now been superseded by the concept of 'special educational needs' (DES, 1978; Gulliford, 1971), a shifting of emphasis which has had a considerable impact on the way in which these pupils are now viewed and provided for. Whereas the medical model attached a convenient label to a child's particular disability, condition or level of functioning and consigned him to a specific category of impairment, or handicap, based on physical or intellectual factors, the concept of special needs liberated the professional from this stereotyped and restrictive mode of thinking and provided a flexible and dynamic alternative. The change of perspective placed the child at the centre of the assessment process rather than at the end of it. No longer was he an interesting case to be identified and labelled and channelled into the system but suddenly, like a butterfuly emerging from a chrysalis, he became an individual in his own right; an individual with his own unique needs.

The implications of his new orientation were, and still are, wide-ranging in terms of both provision and opportunity. For the pupil, the recognition by the team that he has individual needs and hitherto unexplored potential removes any artificially imposed ceiling which labelling might imply, and provides an open-ended opportunity for development. For the professional, it supplants the 'diagnosis, prognosis, treatment' model of 'intervention' with a more eclectic and collaborative model of 'practice'. By focusing on the pupil instead of the diagnosis, a system of restrictive practices is replaced by something of worth. Remove the label and you remove the blindfold. Place the pupil at the centre of the assessment, planning and review process and the value of having the numerous professionals who are responsibile for his education operating as a team is immediately evident.

The purpose of this chapter is to explore some of the issues surrounding the concept of collaborative work which is fundamental to effective inter-disciplinary practice. The advantages of such an approach should be obvious and have been well documented, but there are nevertheless problems which have to be identified and acted upon. However, before considering the difficulties which have to be addressed, a brief review of the evolution of multi-disciplinary and collaborative work will place it within the context of recent legislation and current ideology.

The Court Report (DHSS, 1976) and the Warnock Report (DES, 1978) were instrumental in effecting a significant change in both the working practices and the philosophical alignment of professionals in health, social service and education authorities. The 1981 Education Act (DES, 1981) incorporated the recommendations of both reports and emphasized the importance of a multi-disciplinary approach. The Warnock Report had stated:

> The development of close working relationships between professionals in the different services concerned with children and young people with special needs is central to this report (DES, 1978, 16.1)

a view later endorsed by Circular 1/83 (DES, 1983):

> By bringing together the skills, perceptions and insights of profession-
> als in different disciplines, it should be possible to arrive at a more
> complete understanding (p. 34).

The formal recognition of the existence of some good practice and the
need for wider application encapsulated in the 1981 Act, stemmed not
only from the two reports, but was also a result of a subtle change in
the perceptions of professionals from a number of disciplines. Two
years prior to the publication of the Court Report, the Open
University and produced a sourcebook *The Handicapped Person in
the Community* (Boswell and Wingrove, 1974) which spanned a wide
range of disciplines and agencies involved with handicapped people. It
had been compiled by an interdisciplinary team and provided a
valuable insight into the (as then) unresolved dilemmas facing professionals at the interface of various disciplines. Some vivid examples of
the frustrations and discontent experienced by professionals working
in isolation were presented from a variety of perspectives.
Contributors instanced the lack of collaboration and coordination
within their own disciplines and offered suggestions to remedy some of
the difficulties. Boswell proposed '. . . an examination of professional
roles and ideologies that will encourage an inter-professional
approach to problems' (p. 1); Nichols (1974) suggested that assessment
should be based upon '. . . a complete evaluation of the physical,
functional, educational, psychological and social attainments'
(p. 372); and Kershaw (1974) summarized his appraisal of the situation
as:

> The care of any handicapped child, however minor his disability, is a
> task for a team working in the harmonious relationship which exists
> when members of several disciplines forget 'demarcation lines' and
> professional possessiveness and join in the common pursuit of the total
> aim, ensuring that the child shall have the best possible chance of
> realising all his potentialities (p. 216).

As an ideal, it is virtually unassailable; as a working reality, operated
with goodwill and commitment on all sides, it is achievable. Similarly
the Tunbridge Report (DHSS, 1972) considered the major problems
existing between the remedial professions (physiotherapists, occupational therapists and remedial gymnasts) and identified them as a lack
of role, of definition and of clarity, a marked degree of overlap and
duplication and a general lack of cooperation resulting in poor communication.

The practical obstacles which have to be overcome before these ideals can be translated into effective practice are many and varied, but the successes to be gained are incalculable. The onus is on the special school to orchestrate and promote such an approach. Thomson (1984) puts forward the premise:

> All the professionals have, as a common basis of interest, the child with special needs. The amount of child contact that these professionals have varies, but it is the school which is the agency having most contact with the child and its needs. The school can present to any multidisciplinary situation the most objective, up-to-date information about the child and its needs (p. 120–21).

In her foreword to *Parental Involvement* (Wolfendale, 1989), Glenys Kinnock makes the point that '. . . Schools are places not just for teachers and children but for parents and others from the community' (p. ix) and further suggests that '. . . We have to be prepared to open up our schools and classrooms . . .'. The notion of schools being insular in outlook and practice and needing to 'open up' is an interesting one, particularly given the infrastructure which supports them and the network of agencies with which they are inextricably involved.

Special schools are situated at the centre of a complex pattern of autonomous, yet complementary, systems and services. An often bewildering array of educational, medical, paramedical, psychological and social practitioners are involved, to varying degrees, in the life and work of each institution. Figure 8.1 illustrates the multiplicity of professionals, disciplines and auxiliary personnel which operates within the sphere of special needs; the list is by no means exhaustive.

Freeman and Gray (1989) refer to the 'triangle of provision' representing the three major providers of services for children with special educational needs, namely District Health Authorities, Social Services Department and the Local Education Authorities, and note that

> Headteachers are at the hub of activity in special educational needs, and the burden of responsibility for the management and co-ordination of services within and outside the school falls largely on their shoulders . . . it also falls to the headteacher to liaise with parents, and the various agencies with which the school must deal (p. 114).

It is, therefore, not surprising that the concept of effective multidisciplinary cooperation is seen by some as more of an ideal than a reality:

> The development of extended 'multi-professional assessment, advocated by both the Court and the Warnock reports . . . assumes an

Figure 8.1 Influences on the pupil

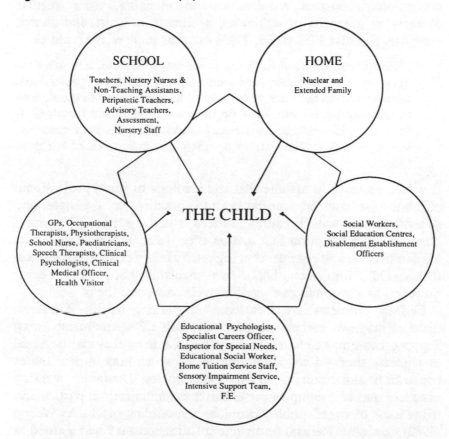

unrealistic degree of communicaiton, co-operation and absence of professional conflicts and jealousies' (Tomlinson, 1982, p. 31)

Nevertheless, such teamwork is undertaken with varying degrees of success.

Collaboration or Conflict?

Problems may occur in the area of inter-disciplinary cooperation. The inter-disciplinary approach uses a team of professionals from different disciplines who share problems and responsibilities in order to work constructively for the benefit of the child. Opportunities for regular interactions and joint planning are prerequisites, but mutual professional respect, willing cooperation and compromise were also essential ingredients. Teamwork of this kind is not an automatic consequence of work undertaken in close promixity to other professionals. Success requires careful planning, using regular contacts as a means of achieving a climate of trust and shared expertise. Circular 1/83 (DES, 1983) outlines some of the realities:

Effective multi-professional work is not easy to achieve. It requires co-operation, collaboration and mutual support. Each professional adviser needs to be aware of the roles of his colleagues and should seek to reach agreement with them on their several roles and functions. It follows from this that his advice should reflect his own concerns, leaving others to concentrate on their particular area of expertise (para. 3).

It would be naive to assume that the ideology of multi-professional collaboration can be translated into practice in a simple and straightforward way. It cannot. Indeed, there are those who would question the assumption that it is as effective as its advocates would have us believe, and consider that the reality falls well short of the ideal (Potts, 1983; Tomlinson, 1982). In recognizing that problems exist, however, professionals can work actively to resolve them.

Certain problems are locational in nature. Health Authority districts may not correspond precisely with LEA catchment areas; support teams may be based over a wide area; therapists may be based at separate sites – a set of circumstances which may impose major constraints and result in serious inefficiencies. Dissimilar working practices may also compromise effective communication, particularly if the issue of confidentiality provides a stumbling block. As Welton (1982) cautions: 'Refusal to divulge information may be regarded as good practice within one profession, but may be misunderstood or resented by another (p. 272).

The key issues are effective communication and an understanding of the different roles and working practices of the members of a multi-disciplinary team. If systems are explained and channels of communication opened up, there are few misunderstandings or misconceptions which cannot be resolved. As Hanko (1985) points out:

Disagreement between professionals occurs, as we know, across as well as within institutions, and can enrich professional life as much as it sometimes frustrates it. Hazards are more likely when there is an insufficient exchange of information and no systematic discussion of experience between colleagues (p. 36).

Personal responses within the context of a multi-disciplinary structure should not be underestimated. Individuals can feel threatened or vulnerable when asked to share their views with professionals who are more experienced or whose values, beliefs or perspectives are different from their own. Mutual trust can be slow to develop and there are those who, for reasons best known to themselves, choose to use their professional status as a barrier. These difficulties may be due to a lack of professional confidence, a defence mechanism to deflect potential criticism or an intrinsic belief in the superiority of one profession over another. The problems of role uncertainty and role overlap are referred to in Coupe and Porter (1986), whilst Fish (1985) makes the observation that: 'Experience would tend to show that a person should be secure in his own professional role if he is to function effectively with others' (p. 123).

The potential for a conflict of interests to arise in any situation which involves a range of professionals is, of course, ever-present (Freeman and Gray, 1989). Conflict, a factor whenever a group of individuals is engaged in a joint activity, is likely to be present in the special school where professional boundaries provide increased potential for tension, particularly when priorities and perspectives may be significantly different (Bowers, 1984). In the chapter on the nature of power, 'Power and conflict: facts of life', Bowers analyses the use of power, defines conflict and suggests ways in which it may be handled. Assertiveness, cooperation and compromise are all explained in detail, and a valuable insight into the skills of conflict management is provided.

Easen (1985) tackles the issue of school-based INSET in an accessible and comprehensive fashion, addressing some of the major concerns and analysing them in practical terms. Considering problems, improving communication, learning through discussion, resolving conflict and supporting change are dealt with.

All members of a multi-disciplinary team bring their own particular skills, expertise and expectations into the collaborative arena, and Hanko (1985) reminds us of the ground-rules for such interactions. She suggests that expertise in itself is not enough. An awareness of the situation within which a particular specialism is to be applied is a prerequisite of successful collaboration (she coins the phrase 'aspects of the landscape') allied to the skilful and flexible use of such expertise:

> Each professional willing to share his understanding with groups of other professionals will have his own way of using it. To do so effectively, however, requires special skills, based on an understanding of the work setting in which they are to be exercised (p. 56).

Adopting a team approach

The arguments for operating an inter-disciplinary approach to the provision of appropriate support and intervention programmes for pupils with a wide range of special needs are persuasive. But how is such an approach to be translated into practice? How is the theory and the underpinning ideology to be transformed into effective action?

The first stage in the process is the intention of 'making it happen'; a shared vision as to what is both possible and desirable. In essence, it is a refinement of the concept of a whole-school approach where an attempt is made 'to utilise all the resources of a school to foster the development of all its children' (Ainscow and Florek, 1989, p. 3). In this instance, it is the coordination of disciplines and skills and personnel, the human resources, in a shared undertaking.

The second stage, the tacit removal of professional barriers, occurs as a natural consequence of the stated intention of working collaboratively. Devising a framework within which the complementary skills of the team can be employed requires joint planning and discussion, including the identification of existing priorities within a school. Any barriers to cooperation can be removed during the collaborative process since, as Cottam (1986) observed:

> if programmes are prepared, instigated and evaluated by all the professionals involved with the child, the animosity which often arises by encroaching on related professional territory is minimised (p. 137).

Creating the appropriate organizational structure through which these jointly-planned programmes and activities are to be delivered is a crucial aspect of the inter-disciplinary process. Planning and evaluation themselves can be time-consuming but other factors need to be taken into consideration. The frequency and duration of activities, the mode of delivery, the availability of staff and resources, coordination and monitoring, and classroom management will all determine the outcome of the process. The ideal situation is outlined by Fish (1985):

> the work of therapists particularly in the fields of speech and physiotherapy, is enhanced where the therapist and the teacher work together . . . . Cooperation is often at its best when therapists work in the classroom and teachers and aides can see what is done and carry on practice programmes in the therapist's absence. It is at its worst when the therapist and the teacher never meet, and treatment and education are seen as two separate, unrelated activities (p. 92).

Examples of good practice are to be found in many special schools catering for pupils with a range of profound and multiple learning difficulties, sensory impairments, communication disorders and physical disabilities. In every case sustained cooperation and team-work with teachers and classroom aides working side by side to support each other and to implement and reinforce the programmes devised by therapists is evident. Special Support Assistants (including Nursery Nurses) are a valued resource in special schools, and the blurring of role definitions in practical situations often leads to the sharing of responsibility for the instruction of individuals and small groups, and for record keeping and report writing.

In a number of schools for pupils with physical disabilities and associated sensory and learning problems an inter-disciplinary approach aimed at increasing functional mobility, independence and concept development is in evidence. The methods used draw on the innovative work being carried out in Hungary (recently trialled in this country at the Birmingham Institute for Conductive Education) and are based on the theory proposed by Luria (1961) that language is the regulator of movement, and actively involves children through a programme of 'rhythmical intention'. Language is seen as an integral part of movement activities, and is used to direct and consolidate the willed movement of the child in order that he becomes an active participant in, as opposed to being merely the passive recipient of, treatment.

This particular approach, sometimes referred to as the Peto Method after its originator, has been subjected to wide exposure in the media during the last five years although, in reality, it has been undertaken in Budapest for several decades. In this country a number of schemes, often referred to as motor-based learning, have been developed, amalgamating aspects of the Hungarian approach with other models of treatment. The programmes are planned on a multidisciplinary basis, usually involving a teacher, a physiotherapist, an occupational therapist and a speech therapist. Purists might argue that, since the Conductive Education approach involves the use of specially trained 'conductors' (staff trained across the spectrum of therapies, including teaching) any attempt to duplicate it using a multi-disciplinary team will merely result in a diluted version which inaccurately reflects the original practice. Nevertheless, the motor-learning programmes which have been developed using similar principles and theoretical constructs have been devised and implemented as part of an evolving and eclectic process, using the multi-professional skills necessary to create a unified and effective programme. In terms of an inter-disciplinary approach it is a success. It has brought the various disciplines together, encouraged joint planning and evaluation, promoted discussion and challenged preconceptions, explored possibilities and, perhaps above all, developed a coherent and cohesive approach for children with motor-learning problems.

In an ideal situation the role of the various therapists is multi-faceted, and there are institutions in which the ideal is being transformed into a reality. In one school, the therapists (occupational, physio, and speech) undertake a wide spectrum of activities which includes:

- individual and group treatment sessions;
- the monitoring of pupils who do not require intensive inputs;
- initial assessments identifying individual needs;
- collaborative work in the classroom;
- an inter-disciplinary review of pupils;
- regular liaison with teaching staff;
- class-based training for teaching staff;
- joint programme planning and evaluation;
- the purchase and maintenance of equipment;
- liaison with parents and home visits;
- contributions to INSET;
- involvement in case conferences and medical examinations.

And this is in no way exhaustive!

Further examples of collaborative multidisciplinary ventures are available. In one school a teacher with responsibility for access work using information technology, carries out a joint assesment with an occupational therapist. The aim is to provide pupils whose fine-motor skills are restricted with modified access devices or switches to allow them to benefit from the use of a computer. The availability of the correct postural aids is essential when pupils are being assessed for specific equipment, and the advice and guidance of staff with the relevant expertise is obviously vital.

As special schools provide a major focus for inter-disciplinary involvement, it is hardly surprising that strong links should have developed which embrace all the complementary disciplines and facilitate new and innovative ways of delivering the necessary services and curricula. These initiatives, however, may be restricted to the school setting, and not accepted as general practice within the whole of an LEA.

It is encouraging to note that INSET courses are being offered which recognize and address the need for collaborative work across the professions and, in particular, across the therapies. The most recent example relates to the Education Support Grant (ESG) which the DES has specified for the purchase of special equipment for pupils with communication disorders. The allocation of ESG funding is also intended to meet the training needs of staff involved, thereby establishing a system of support within schools which will be self-renewing and long-term. At least one LEA has suggested that the team be comprised of a teacher, an occupational therapist and a speech therapist, thereby recognizing and endorsing the team approach.

Successful collaboration, however, is not restricted to therapists working with teachers and classroom assistants. It spans the whole range of interactions both in, and beyond, the school. One LEA is piloting a jointly-funded project aimed a providing long-term support for pupils and their families where challenging behaviours and a range of interpersonal problems have significantly affected their quality of life. The Intensive Support Team, composed of educational psychologists and key workers, adopts behaviour management strategies to resolve the range of problems which they encounter, and this necessitates negotiating fully with the client, the family, the school and respite care staff, social workers and others closely involved. Rather than the 'hit-and-run' approach usually associated with over-worked professionals seeking to employ intervention and support programmes, the team is committed to working intensively with the family for as long as it takes to achieve a positive outcome, which the deliberately small caseload makes possible. The approach has yielded remarkable results, and confirms the benefits of a team approach.

Working Collaboratively with Parents

Essential elements in the multi-disciplinary approach are parental involvement and parental partnership. While the title of this chapter implies a multi-professional perspective, the place of parents within the collaborative process has long been recognized. As part of its contribution to the developing philosophy of special education, envisaged by the Warnock Report and encapsulated in the 1981 Education Act, the National Council for Special Education produced a series of pamphlets intended to promote the discussion of a range of issues stemming directly from the new legislation. In the second publication, *Partnership with Parents* Mittler and Mittler (1982) wrote:

> The development of better working relationships between parents and professionals constitutes one of the most significant developments in the field of special education during the last decade (p. 7).

The rationale for the involvement of parents is based on several factors. The Warnock Report (DES, 1978) states that,

> the successful education of children with special needs is dependent on the full involvement of their parents . . . unless parents are seen as equal partners in the education process the purpose of our report will be frustrated (9.1)

This view is echoed by other writers (Cunningham and Davies, 1985; Wolfendale, 1989). 'Research into parental support would seem to suggest that parents are the key educators of children', observe Freeman and Gray (1989, p. 71). They comment, in particular, on the work of Howe (1988) whose research indicated that an intensive educational input by parents for the benefit of their children had a tendency to accelerate their performance in the early years. They also add that 'It is in the teacher's interests to involve parents', a point endorsed by Mittler and Mittler (1982):

> A commitment to partnership rests on the assumption that children will develop and learn better if parents and professionals are working together on a basis of equality than if either are working in isolation (p. 7).

As with the concept of multi-disciplinary involvement and collaboration, the reality of parental partnership has been questioned, with Potts (1983) suggesting that the premise of equal partnership may be more a case of rhetoric than reality. A close examination of the terminology used indicates that there is a need for a definition of terms, and that a distinction should be made between the notion of parental 'involvement' and parental 'partnership'. The latter, argues Marra (1984), is a worthwhile ideal towards which professionals should aspire in their work with parents. It is, by definition, a two-way process, a dialogue between equals, and stems from an acceptance by both parties, parents and professionals, that each has something of worth to offer. Involvement, conversely, can be used to identify virtually any interaction with parents, however incidental or superficial.

Cunningham and Davies (1985) outline three approaches adopted by professionals in their work with parents, in effect a continuum of involvement, characterized by the degree of control exerted by the professional group. The expert model relegates parents to the role of recipients of the expertise invested in the professionals: the flow of information is tightly controlled; confidentiality is maintained; and all the decisions are made by the professional as the acknowledged expert. The transplant model, by contrast, is less autocratic in its approach, although the information is still controlled and decisions are still taken by the professionals. Parents are seen as a useful resource and acquire key skills in order to act as instructors, using the tools provided by the consultant. The consumer model views the parents in a different light: they are seen as having rights, are involved in the negotiations, and are allowed to select from the options available.

If parents are to be full partners within the educational process and seen as 'an integral part of the multi-disciplinary team where the aim is to promote the quality of life of the handicapped child' (McConachie, 1986, p. 264), a commitment on the part of the school must ensure practical and effective mechanisms to make such a contract work. As Marra (1984) states, 'without a continuous and constructive dialogue between parents and teachers, the concept of parental involvement cannot be considered' (p. 135).

Authors such as Freeman and Gray (1988) see parental involvement in terms of a developmental process which evolves over a period of time through various levels of interaction. The most basic level is where parents are tolerated in activities such as fund-raising, but are otherwise seen as something of a nuisance. The next stage in the process presupposes some degree of involvement, usually closely supervised, with access to relevant information. The subsequent level of progression allows a measure of consultation and some involvement in minor decisions, with additional information about teaching programmes and approaches. The fourth, and final stage, is that of parental partnership: participation in the decision-making process is given to the parents and information is unrestricted. The four levels start from the position of 'threat', progress through those of 'invitation' and 'recognition' and culminate in the democratic level of 'rights'. But, as the authors warn,

> the jump from recognition to a rights level is large, and presents major problems for most schools if they have reached the level of recognition that parents have an importance in schooling (p. 74).

The need for a comprehensive model for parent participation was recognized by Hornby (1989) in a proposed framework which could inform practice, and he provides a theoretical hierarchy based on the identified needs and strengths of parents (Figure 8.2). He suggests that,

Figure 8.2 The needs and strengths of parents

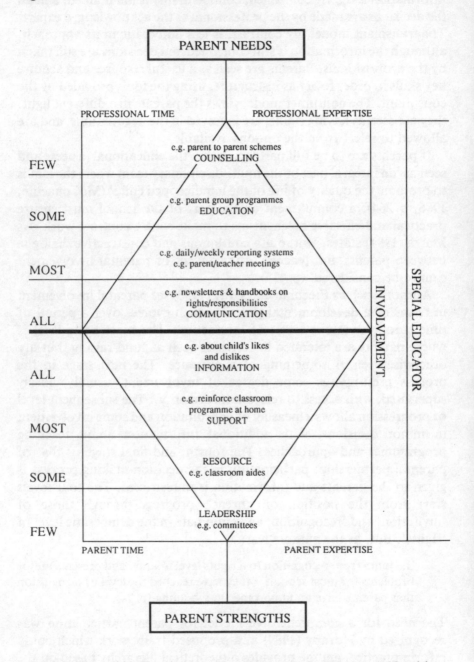

Source: Hornby, G. (1989) 'A model of parent participation', *British Journal of Special Education*, 16, 4, p. 161.

while all parents have some needs and some strengths which can be drawn upon, professionals will have to spend more time and expertise on those few parents who have an intense need for guidance or who will make an extensive contribution (p. 161).

Whilst schools vary in the degree to which they actively seek to involve parents, and there is, undoubtedly, a level of resistance in some quarters, there can be no denying that the question of parental involvement is on the agenda of every mainstream establishment, particularly since the introduction of local management has encouraged an element of competition between schools. Within the sphere of special needs, however, the concept of working closely with parents is generally well-established as part of the ethos of the school. Most schools would admit that there is still much to do before the reality of partnership is fully integrated into their practice.

Since special schools are dealing with pupils with recognised special needs and their families, the general climate tends to be one of support and an acknowledged level of cooperation, however tentative. Thus, the majority of schools have a range of strategies for involving and communicating with parents. Home-school diaries, newsletters, formal and informal meetings between parents and staff, school medicals, annual reports, parent workshops and careers conferences are just a few of the mechanisms which schools have introduced to ensure an ongoing dialogue with parents. The barriers to interaction and collaboration are gradually being eroded.

There will always be difficulties to overcome and no school can afford to be complacent. An investment of time and effort is required if true inter-disciplinary involvement is to be established, and the same is true of parental involvement and partnership initiatives. Mittler and Mittler (1982) identify five factors as intrinsic to the process of partnership: mutual respect and the recognition of equality; the sharing of skills and information; the process of sharing; a joint role in decision-making; and, finally, the recognition of the individuality of families and the uniqueness of the child with special needs; all serve to strengthen and develop the partnership between professionals.

Concluding her overview of partnership models between parents and teachers, Hanko (1985) writes:

A picture ... emerges of well-intentioned efforts and of obstacles to be overcome if a parent-teacher partnership is to achieve the conjoint support which children's special needs might require (p. 98).

The same could be said of multi-disciplinary relationships. The essential question to pose in considering all multi-disciplinary initiatives, whether between parents and professionals or on an inter-disciplinary scale, would seem to be not 'should we?' but rather 'how can we...?'

Note

The author wishes to thank the Editor of *British Journal of Special Education* and Garry Hornby for their kind permission to include Figure 8.2, from 'A model of parent participation' (16, 4, December 1989, p. 161).

References

Ainscow, M. and Florek, A. (1989) *Special Educational Needs: Towards a Whole School Approach*. London: David Fulton in association with NCSE.

Boswell, D. M. and Wingrove, J. M. (Eds) (1974) *The Handicapped Person in the Community*. London: Tavistock in association with the Open University.

Bowers, T. (1984) 'Power and conflict: Facts of life', in Bowers, T. (Ed.) *Management and the Special School*. London: Croom Helm.

Burnham, M. and Brayton, H. (1988) *Working in Special Schools*. Oxford: OPTIS.

Cottam, P. (1986) 'An approach for the mentally handicapped?', in Cottam, P. and Sutton, A. (Eds) *Conductive Education: A System for Overcoming Motor Disorders*. London: Croom Helm.

Coupe, S. and Porter, J. (1986) *The Education of Children with Severe Learning Difficulties. Bridging the Gap between Theory and Practice*. Beckenham: Croom Helm.

Cunningham, C. and Davies, H. (1985) *Working with Parents*. Milton Keynes: Open University Press.

Department of Education and Science (1978) *Special Educational Needs* (The Warnock Report). London: HMSO.

Department of Education and Science (1981) *The Education Act 1981* London: HMSO.

Department of Education and Science (1983) *Assessments and Statements of Special Educational Needs* (Circular 1/83). (Joint circular with the DHSS: Health Circular HC (83/3).) London: HMSO.

Department of Health and Social Services Welsh Office, Central Health Services Council (1972) *Rehabilitation: Report of a Sub-Committee of the Standing Medical Advisory Committee* (The Tunbridge Report). London: HMSO.

Department of Health and Social Services (1976) *Fit for the Future* (The Court Report). London: HMSO.

Easen, P. (1985) *Making School-centred INSET Work*. Milton Keynes: The Open University in association with Croom Helm.

Fish, J. (1985) *Special Education: The Way Ahead*. Milton Keynes: Open University Press.

Freeman, A. and Gray, H. (1989) *Organising Special Educational Needs: A Critical Approach*. London: Paul Chapman.

Gulliford, R. (1971) *Special Educational Needs*. London: Routledge and Kegan Paul.

Hanko, G. (1985) *Special Needs in Ordinary Classrooms*. Oxford: Basil Blackwell.

Hornby, G. (1989) 'A model for parent participation', *British Journal of Special Education*, 16, 4, pp. 161–2.

Howe, M. (1988) ' "Hothouse" children', *The Psychologist*, 1, 9, pp. 356–8.

Kershaw, J. D. (1974) 'Handicapped children in the ordinary school', in Boswell, D. M. and Wingrove, J. M. (Eds) *The Handicapped Person in the Community*. London: Tavistock in association with the Open University.

Luria, A. R. (1961) *The Role of Speech in the Regulation of Normal and Abnormal Behaviour* (Ed. J. Tizard). Oxford: Pergamon.

Marra, M. (1984) 'Parents of children with moderate learning difficulties', in Bowers, T. (Ed.) *Management and the Special School*. London: Croom Helm.

Mittler, P. and Mittler, H. (1982) *Partnership with Parents*. Stratford: NCSE.

McConachie, H. (1986) 'Parents' contribution to the education of their child', in Coupe, J. and Porter, J. (Eds) *The Education of Children with Severe Learning Difficulties. Bridging the Gap between Theory and Practice*. London: Croom Helm.

Nichols, P. J. R. (1974) 'Assessment of the severely disabled', in Boswell, D. M. and Wingrove, J. M. (Eds) *The Handicapped Person in the Community*. London: Tavistock in association with the Open University.

Potts, P. (1983) 'What difference would integration make to the professionals?', in Booth, T. and Potts, P. (Eds) *Integrating Special Education*. Oxford: Basil Blackwell.

Thomson, V. (1984) 'Links with other professionals: the head as a multidisciplinary team member', in Bowers, T. (Ed.) *Management and the Special School*. London: Croom Helm.

Tomlinson, S. (1982) *A Sociology of Special Education*. London: Routledge and Kegan Paul.

Welton, J. (1982) 'Schools in a welfare network', *Child Care, Health and Development*, 8, 271–82.

Wolfendale, S. (Ed.) (1989) *Parental Involvement: Developing Networks Between School, Home and Community*. London: Cassell.

CHAPTER 9

Classroom Evaluation

Christina Tilstone

Early attempts to provide a working definition for classroom evaluation were not wholly successful. In the 1960s, the Schools Council's research programme concentrated on ways in which in-service courses for teachers could be improved. The underlying assumptions were that such changes would automatically result in improvements in the quality of education available for pupils. Work undertaken in the USA during the same period had similar limitations, with an emphasis on narrowly-defined goals and the values of objective measurement and testing, as in the UK.

Recent developments have focused on evaluation as a process of enquiry into the curriculum as it is being achieved, with special emphasis on the learning experiences provided for children. This view of curriculum evaluation encompasses what should be taught and what is learned. Ainscow and Tweddle (1988) emphasize that a broader perspective is essential and that teachers should consider evaluation as an analysis not only of objectives, but of tasks and activities and classroom arrangements: 'Evaluation is a continuous process which involves reflecting upon and interpreting events and activities in the classroom, as they happen' (p. 19).

It should be emphasized, however, that much of what is essential in the education of pupils with severe learning difficulties can, and does, take place outside the 'formal' classroom situation. Teaching and learning often capitalize upon 'natural settings': the corridor, the dining room, the bathroom and the school bus. But learning also happens when teachers do not lead or intervene, and if a pupil is 'shadowed' over a prolonged period the influence and power of the hidden curriculum is appreciated. Hargreaves (1982) identified the hidden curriculum as the events and situations which are not planned nor intended by teachers, but which communicate hidden messages concerning attitudes and values to their pupils. One of Hargreaves' concerns was the unconscious and unintended actions of school staff. His research revealed that disadvantaged pupils in mainstream schools often experienced the destruction of their dignity during their school life. Therefore care is needed to ensure that the dignity of pupils with severe learning difficulties is preserved at all times and that the hidden curriculum comes under the same close scrutiny as the intended one. Candappa and Burgess (1989), in a penetrating investigation of ways in which the attitudes of carers influence the self-image of people with severe learning difficulties, found that in a hospital setting many staff were unaware of the negative attitudes which they displayed in unguarded moments. The results were the development of a relationship of dependency and 'for some clients' the destruction of positive self images. In McCormick and James' (1983) account of curriculum evaluation, the intended, the actual and the hidden curriculum as experienced by pupils are considered in some detail. Their conclusions are concerned with the outcomes of learning in terms of the values and attitudes which pupils develop through all their experiences.

The booklet *Quality in Schools: Evaluation and Appraisal* (DES 1985) suggests that the following are essential elements in evaluation:

Assessment – implies measurement and grading based on known criteria.

Review – indicates a retrospective activity and implies the collection and examination of evidence and information.

Appraisal – emphasizes the forming of qualitative judgements about an activity, a person, or an organization.

Evaluation – a general term used to denote a systematic study, undertaken by an institution or a Local Education Authority, of the quality of the educational provision.

The document considers all four as discrete elements, but Holly and Wally (1989) regard assessment, review and appraisal as major interrelated parts of the evaluation process, a view shared by the present author. Figure 9.1 demonstrates ways in which the parts interconnect.

118

Figure 9.1 The continuing process of evaluation

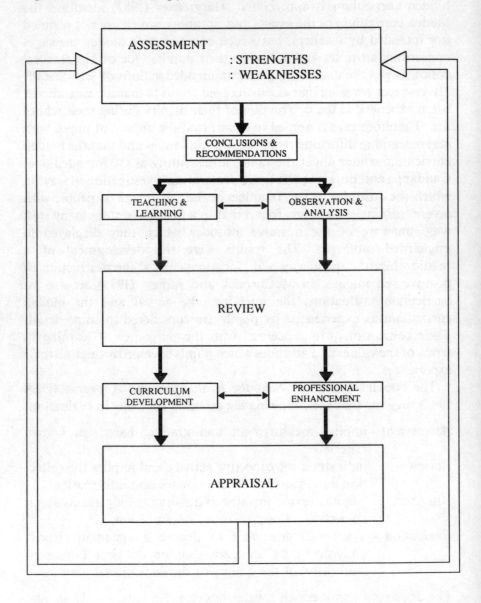

Assessment

Assessment is the first element in this evaluative process and is concerned with the identification of a child's strengths and weaknesses in particular environments and situations. In the 1960s, when pupils with severe learning difficulties were the responsibility of the Local

Health Authorities, the term had strong medical connotations which involved the diagnosis of the abnormal condition and the identification of the consequent handicap. This definition resulted in stereotyping and labelling, a situation of concern to the Warnock Committee and which teachers are still challenging today. For example, the fact that a pupil is diagnosed as having Down's syndrome is relatively unimportant within the context of the curriculum; what is of importance, however, is whether or not he can communicate with others or dress himself. It is essential that teachers concentrate their assessment on all areas of development: intellectual, physical, sensory, social and emotional. Credit should be given for what the child can do, rather than emphasizing what he cannot do. Obviously, the teacher needs a good grasp of assessment techniques but of equal importance are her own observations of the child's response to stimuli in context over a period of time. Johnson (1986) states that assessment techniques 'are of most use in testing hypotheses rather than general curriculum ideas' (p. 283).

It is the teacher's observations of a child's interactions with his environment (including objects, situations and people), recorded on many occasions, which may present clues to the relevance of curriculum content and delivery. Assessment must be detailed and comprehensive, and will rightly lead to informed judgements which can be used as a basis for recommendations on what the child needs to learn and what the teacher needs to teach. It is apparent that all children do not learn in the same way and that in order to aid learning a range of strategies needs to be considered.

Teaching and learning

The aims of education should be kept in mind when selecting the learning activities to be presented to pupils with severe learning difficulties; there is no room for irrelevant teaching based on personal preferences. The delivery of the curriculum is dependent not only on the school and the teacher, but on the resources available. This is not a new dilemma, but with substantial cuts in funding the defined curriculum is in danger of becoming 'resources-led' rather than 'needs-led.'

The teacher is a practical theoriser and implicit theories are generated by perceptions of what 'works' in the classroom. (Ashton *et al.*, 1983; Ashton *et al.*, 1989; Peacock and Tilstone, 1991). In practice, personal theories become the basis for subsequent teaching, and are consequently not articulated or challenged as it is usually difficult to state the reason for a particular course of action. Schon (1983) comments that teachers may find themselves at a loss, or produce descriptions that are obviously inappropriate and suggests that their knowledge is in their actions.

Pupils are often engaged in classroom activities because it is the will of the teacher, but without any real understanding of what they are doing or why (Ainscow and Tweddle, 1988). Current initiatives in the field of severe learning difficulties allow pupils to become genuine partners through the discussion and negotiation of curriculum issues – a process which has resulted in pupils taking on more responsibility for their learning and consequently reducing their dependency on their teachers.

If a dynamic curriculum, responsive to changing needs, is to be devised and implemented, both teacher and pupil should be involved in deciding:

- what is to be taught;
- what teaching methods and procedures are to be adopted;
- what resources are needed and how they are to be managed;
- how pupils are to be grouped and how behaviour is to be guided;
- ways in which classroom staff are coordinated and how time is organized.

Observation and analysis

If teachers are to respond to children's changing needs within the context of the curriculum on offer, the ability to observe accurately is essential. Observation is an undervalued skill in teaching. Initial B.Ed. training courses are at last beginning to include observation as an element within the syllabus but it is rarely treated adequately on in-service training courses for teachers. Detailed observation relies on practice, requires concentration and the ability to record accurately what is happening. Good and Brophy (1978) emphasize that teachers are often totally unaware of what is actually happening in their classrooms and either describe events as behaviours which they expect to happen, or miss important signals. They comment, 'if you don't know how to look, you don't see very much' (p. 31). The techniques of observation can be placed in two main categories: those which identify what has been learned (the product) and those which focus on how the learning has taken place (the process).

Techniques used to identify 'the product'

There are two main approaches: event recording and duration recording. Both require the focus of observation to be clearly defined. Event recording (or frequency counts) requires a teacher to record, using a simple tally system, the number of times a child, (or a group of children) gives a specific response.

> Elizabeth wants to investigate the number of times two pupils take turns during the day. She chooses to observe these children at a time when turn-taking is most likely to occur: at the mid-morning break, in the play-ground, at lunch time, and during a Veronica Sherborne movement lesson. She records each of these sessions over a period of one month, analyses the data, and then decides on an action – in this case to create more opportunities for turn-taking in other areas of the curriculum.

Duration recording is a technique used to determine the length of actions or behaviours, and a stop watch is required for accuracy (Cartwright and Cartwright, 1974).

> The focus of investigation is the PE session. Sheila is concerned that not all the activities she had planned were achieved as it appeared that the children took an excessive length of time to undress and put on their PE kit. Over a six-week period she systematically observed and recorded, using a stopwatch, the length of time taken to dress and undress. Her findings confirmed her suspicions. She then decided on the following course of action.
> 1. children will be given more opportunities in meaningful situations to dress and undress;
> 2. the more-able children will be paired with the less-able and encouraged to help with one aspect only of the dressing/undressing process. This will encourage the more-able to take on some responsibility for their less-able peers. The less-able, however, will not be denied the opportunity for some independence.

Techniques which focus on the process

Continuous recording is the one most frequently used by classroom staff. Despite the obvious advantages, there can be difficulties in achieving accurate observation and detailed analysis of the data collected. Video equipment is an invaluable aid, but the time-consuming task of interpreting lengthy tapes can be formidable. Short sessions of continuous observation and recording are extremely useful and relatively easy to facilitate, provided that a focus is specified.

> Olive wants to investigate how one of her pupils, with a severe sensory loss, is learning to play with objects. Does he find them for himself? If so, does he have a favourite? What does he do with it? What happens when he becomes familiar with it? These are all legitimate questions to which she needs answers. She chooses to record everything he does during the same 10-minute period each day at a time when he has the maximum opportunity to be exposed to a range of objects.

She could, of course, choose to video his responses, but the obvious advantages have to be balanced against the expense and the time taken to ensure that equipment is available, working, and in the right place at the right time. If video-recording is to be used, children must be allowed time to get used to the equipment. Many children 'play to the camera' and, in a small scale study of pupils with a range of sensory losses, it was found that some children reacted to the equipment by demonstrating abnormal behaviours. Some were neutral or totally passive; others displayed an exceptional number of startled responses (Tilstone, 1989).

Time-sampling and interval-recording are flexible techniques which can be used to analyse both the process and the product. Time-sampling enables the teacher to observe and record the events and interactions at regular intervals throughout the school day; on the hour, for example. Although the method can only focus on isolated elements of work in progress, and may be seen as partial and limited, the data collected can be invaluable in subsequent planning. Interval-recording requires the teacher to estimate the total time that she can devote to observation and then to apportion it in equal parts throughout the school day. For example, the teacher might decide to observe and record for five minutes during each hour. Interval-recording enables a stream of actions, behaviours and events to be documented.

The emphasis in this chapter, so far, has been on the need for observation and on the techniques available to the teacher. In order to evaluate classroom practice effectively, however, teachers need a frame of reference. Some reconstruct events by using tight observation schedules; others use simple 'field notes' or 'nudge sheets' as aides-mémoire (Bailey, 1991).

A proven model is the Open University In-service Education pack Curriculum in Action (Ashton et al., 1980). Devised by mainstream teachers keen to improve their classroom practice, the self-contained pack includes four blocks of material which are intended to develop a teacher's evaluation skills. The work undertaken is determined by the answers to six basic questions:

> What did the pupils actually do?
> What were they learning?
> How worthwhile was it?
> What did I do?
> What did I learn?
> What do I intend to do now? (Block 1, p. 11).

Teachers of pupils with severe learning difficulties have found the pack invaluable when they rigorously examine their classroom practices in order to evolve a relevant curriculum. One teacher commented, 'This (pack), I found, was very exciting and challenging, and has helped me to develop a practical curriculum based on the exact needs of my children'.

In order to evaluate classroom practice effectively it is important to focus on one aspect of the curriculum at a time. The areas or issues chosen for investigation should, in the teacher's opinion, be those which are of priority for her in her own teaching, whether involving individual pupils or groups.

> Mary, for example, wanted to investigate whether or not one pupil with profound multiple learning difficulties interacted in any way with his peers when there was no deliberate teacher intervention. She hoped that the results would enable her to provide him with better methods of indicating his needs and wants. Lorraine, on the other hand, was keen to examine whether the content of her life-skills programme was being taught in a way which encouraged group cooperation, as well as the achievement of individual skills.

Both teachers used the six questions from the *Curriculum in Action* pack. They recorded what the pupils did in order to ascertain what they might have learned. It is difficult to be confident about the learning that has taken place but, by observing and recording over a period, it is possible to reach an informed opinion. These two teachers discovered that stringent observation and the processing of the data recorded led them to consider the third and most important curriculum-in-action question, 'How worthwhile was it?'. It is often difficult for teachers to determine priorities within a curriculum which allows pupils to make an active and positive contribution to society. The criteria for this prioritizing process depend upon the teacher's personal agenda. 'How worthwhile was it?' is a necessary question.

The enquiry however, may prove to be threatening, as it can lead not only to changes in content, but also to changes in well-established and highly valued teaching styles and routines. It may be particularly difficult for teachers to accept that many day-to-day practices, including the short-cutting of self-help skills when time is limited, have been developed in order to survive and are irrelevant to the education of pupils. Woods (1990) reminds us that:

> A feature of successful survival strategies is their permanence and ongoing refinement. They contain the seeds of their own continuance and growth, often outliving their usefulness, and festering, causing another problem for which survival strategy must be devised. They do not take a problem out of the arena, as it were, leaving more for teaching. Rather they expand into teaching and around it, like some parasitic plant, and eventually in some cases the host might be completely killed off (p. 97).

In some cases, however, after evaluating the learning experience that she is presenting, a teacher may decide that no changes are necessary as each pupil is benefiting to the full. This is an unlikely conclusion, as teaching is both complex and fluid, and teachers need to face new challenges daily. The implementation of the National Curriculum, for example, has brought about conflicts between practicalities, personal ideals and wider educational concerns, all of which need to be considered and resolved in the classroom. If teaching is to incorporate new principles, teachers must have the opportunities to reflect on their current practices.

Review

Progress in evaluating the curriculum depends on much more than commitment and the will to change; it also requires reflection. 'Critical reflection on the systematic evidence gathered should be an integral part of the teacher's life in school' (Pollard and Tann, 1987). The term 'reflective teachers' is useful and popular but Easen (1985), in his highly practical and enlightening book *Making School-centred INSET Work*, uses a more precise and functional term: 'reflecting teachers'. These are teachers who identify their 'limits' and find ways of reaching beyond them; teachers who establish an inner dialogue between the action taken and the reflections made; teachers who establish their own vision for their own practice. This vision will naturally be formed by the systematic gathering and analysis of evidence. Eason's notion of reflecting teachers can be likened to the Piagetian concept of development, when concrete experiences are reflected upon, assimilated, accommodated and extended into further action. It is possible, with commitment and practice, for a teacher to carry out curriculum evaluation on her own, as outlined in this chapter. Teachers of pupils with severe learning difficulties, however, rarely work alone. The majority are closely involved with special support assistants or are engaged in team-teaching. Even simple adjustments to timetables can lead to the development of fruitful partnerships. The partner can offer an additional perspective and is able with careful planning to sustain observation over an agreed period. She needs to be as involved as the teacher in order to comment critically on what is actually happening, as she too may have stereotyped theories about teaching and learning. A major benefit of the partnership approach is that the observer can, through analysis and interpretation, deepen the teacher's understanding of those aspects of her teaching which are under review.

A further possibility is the participation of a teacher colleague from another class (sometimes termed 'a critical friend'), who is willing to share experiences and to offer mutual support. To work effectively, such a scheme requires the encouragement of the head teacher and the senior management team. Relief teaching will be needed if teachers are to visit each other's classrooms, and time should be allowed for post-observation discussions. These arrangements have proved highly cost-effective methods of ensuring real and relevant curriculum review and development.

Teacher/outsider partnerships are also feasible. May and Sigsworth (1982; 1988) argue persuasively for the benefits of such arrangements. In the main, 'outsiders' are researchers or college lecturers who have been invited to assist in curriculum development. The possibilities are exciting, but success will depend on the willingness of a teacher to trust a partial stranger.

Curriculum development and professional enhancement

By inquiring into the curriculum experienced by the pupils and constantly questioning its relevance, it is unlikely that the curriculum will remain the same. Changes in learning, however, can only be implemented through changes to the actions which affect that learning. Thus, the teacher, who is genuine facilitator, continues her own education alongside that of her pupils. These parallel processes are possible only when she allows the information collected to become the basis for informed and improved action (Nias and Groundwater-Smith, 1988). Although teachers who are 'taking stock' of their work are involved in a form of self-evaluation, dynamic curriculum development and delivery can best be achieved through a comprehensive and creative programme of in-service training. A major part of the continuous professional development of teachers depends upon their own ability to enquire into, and challenge, their own practices and a whole-school policy is essential.

Appraisal

The final stage in the evaluation cycle is appraisal. Shostak (1987) emphasizes that there is a tendency to view appraisal in terms of accountability, 'a process which could be used to eliminate incompetence' (p. 142). He argues that as appraisal can be seen to have direct links with conditions of service and with career prospects, its effect on professional development can easily be overlooked. Teachers will now be required to take part in appraisal, but it should be stressed that this situation is not new. Bell (1988) states that the initial criteria, defined by inspectors of schools in the middle of the nineteenth century, included 'gentleness and piety'. The 1976 Ruskin College speech of James Callaghan stressed the need for the curriculum to be placed under public scrutiny and for teachers to become accountable to society at large. Teachers' attitudes towards appraisal are determined not only by their own perceptions and fears, but also by the attitudes of parents, industry and commerce to teaching and teaching standards.

DES (1990) documents have stressed that appraisal should not be seen as a threat, but as a series of opportunities to allow teachers to establish their professional status. Bell (1988), writing before schools were recommended to introduce teacher appraisal, stressed that it should stem from, and be compatible with, the particular circumstances of a school. Pilot studies have shown that if teachers want appraisal schemes which match their own needs and principles, they need to be involved in all parts of the process (Bunnell and Stephens, 1984). Special schools were poorly represented in these studies, although Pardoe and Attfield (1989) give an enlightened account of their own schools' involvement in the Salford scheme. Both are heads of special schools: one for pupils with severe learning difficulties; the other for pupils with a range of learning difficulties. The basic principle of the schemes was the use of self-evaluation as a key element in appraisal, but using a 'support teacher' to help in the process. Information, agreed upon by teachers, was made available to the appraisers (the head-teachers or their deputies), as a basis for the appraisal interview.

Williams and Petrie (1989) suggest guidelines for appraisal in special schools, based on a small-scale survey in the north-west of England. They emphasize the need to recognize the value of cooperative approaches, at the same time encouraging teachers to examine their own teaching self-critically in order to encourage professional growth. They also underline the view that appraisal should be extended to all members of the multi-disciplinary team who provide support to the school.

Since the introduction of appraisal as a legal requirement, many Local Education Authorities have developed frameworks designed to foster honesty and effective communication in order to encourage staff to achieve ownership of the process. Wiltshire LEA has developed a model for special schools which is based on detailed discussions, involving staff, on the aims of schools, their organizational needs, and the demands of the curriculum. This, in turn, determines the professional development plans for each individual teacher.

The DES letter of 10 December 1990 to the Chief Education Officers in England and Wales, stresses that appraisal schemes for teachers will form part of their normal working life in order to enhance their professional skills and hence improve the education of their pupils. In an Annex to the letter, the Secretary of State emphasizes that the schemes shall be designed to help and support teachers, in a continuous, systematic way. The debate, however, continues.

Conclusions

The sixth question of *Curriculum in Action* (Ashton *et al.*, 1980) is 'What do I intend to do now?' The answer is of course, 'Start the evaluation process again', for classroom evaluation is a continuous process which should be built into the every-day life of the school. If teachers are serious about improving the learning experiences offered to their pupils, they, too, must learn from their pupils' responses to their actions.

128

References

Ainscow, M. and Tweddle, D. A. (1988) *Encouraging Classroom Success*. London: David Fulton.

Ashton, P. M. E., Henderson, E. S. and Peacock, A. (1989) *Teacher Education through Evaluation: The principles and practice of IT-INSET* London: Routledge.

Ashton, P. M. E., Hunt, P., Jones, S. and Watson, G. (1980) *Curriculum in Action: An Approach to Evaluation*. Milton Keynes: Open University Press.

Bailey, T. (1991) 'Classroom observation: A powerful tool for teachers', *Support for Learning* 6, 1, pp. 32–6.

Bell, L. (1988) *Appraising Teachers in Schools. A Practical Guide*. London: Routledge.

Bunnell, S. and Stephens, E. (1984) 'Teacher appraisal – a democratic approach', *School Organisation*, 4, 4, pp. 291–302.

Candappa, M. and Burgess, R. (1989) *'I'm not handicapped – I'm different: Normalization; hospital care and mental handicap'*, in Barton, L. (Ed.) *Disability and Dependency*. London: Falmer Press.

Cartwright, C. A. and Cartwright, C. P. (1974) *Developing Observation Skills*. London: McGraw.

Department of Education and Science (1985) *Quality in Schools: Evaluation and Appraisal, An HMI Study*. London: HMSO.

Department of Education and Science (1990) 'Teacher appraisal: Policy and education support', Grant letter to Chief Education Officers of LEAs in England, 10 December 1990.

Easen, P. (1985) *Making School-centred INSET Work*. London: Croom Helm.

Good, T. L. and Brophy, J. E. (1978) *Looking in Classrooms*, 2nd edn. New York: Harper Row.

Hargreaves, D. (1979) 'A phenomenological approach to classroom decision making', in Eggleton, J. (Ed.) *Teacher Decision-making in the Classroom*. London: Routledge & Kegan, Paul.

Hargreaves, D. (1982) *The Challenge for the Comprehensive School Culture, Curriculum and Community*. London: Routledge & Kegan Paul.

Holly, M. L. H. and Wally, C. (1989) 'Teachers as professionals', in Holly, M. L. H. and McLoughlin, C. (Eds) *Perspectives on Teacher Professional Development*. London: Falmer Press.

Johnson, M. (1986) 'The role of school staff', in Coupe, J. and Porter, J. (Eds) *The Education of Children with Severe Learning Difficulties*. London: Croom Helm.

McCormick, R. and James, M. (1983) *Curriculum Evaluation in Schools*. London: Croom Helm.

May, N. and Sigsworth, A. (1982) 'Teacher-outsider partnership in the observation of classrooms', in Ruddick, J. (Ed.) *Teachers in Partnership. Four Studies in In-Service Collaboration*. Schools Council Programme. York: Longmans.

May, N. and Sigsworth, A. (1988) 'Teacher-outsider partnership in the observation of classrooms', in Murphy, R. and Torrance, H. (Eds) *Evaluating Education Issues and Methods*. London: Harper Row.

Nias, J. and Groundwater-Smith, S. (Eds) (1988) *The Enquiring Teacher*. London: Falmer Press.

Pardoe, J. and Attfield, R. (1989) 'Appraisal: The Salford experience', *British Journal of Special Education*, 16, 3, pp. 103–5.

Peacock, A. and Tilstone, C. (1991) 'IT-INSET and special education', in Upton, G. (Ed.) *Staff Training and Special Educational Needs: Innovatory Strategies and Models of Delivery*. London: David Fulton.

Pollard, A. and Tann, S. (1987) *Reflective Teaching in the Primary School*. London: Cassell.

Schon, D. (1983) *The Reflective Practitioner. How Professionals Think in Action*. New York: Basic Books.

Shostak, R. (1987) 'The role and practice of evaluation in Local Education Authorities...so what?', in Murphy, R. and Torrance, H. (Eds) *Evaluation and Education: Issues and Methods*. London: Harper Row.

Tilstone, C. (1989) 'Methods of observing PMLD children', *PMLD Link*, 4 pp. 1–3.

Williams, K. and Petrie, I. (1989) 'Teacher appraisal in special schools', *British Journal of Special Education*, 16, 2, pp. 53–6.

Woods, P. (1990) *Teacher Skills and Strategies*. London: Falmer Press.

CHAPTER 10

The Class Teacher and Stress

Christina Tilstone

Teaching is undoubtedly a stressful profession. The complex interplay of skills, knowledge, interactions, experiences and the constant need to encourage positive attitudes make it physically, emotionally and mentally demanding. Some intending teachers opt out during training, but once trained their commitment is, in the main, strong. It has been suggested that the traumas of degree courses and experiences during the first few years in the classroom are the equivalent of an initiation rite, the successful survival of which becomes a matter of pride (Hargreaves and Woods, 1984). However, pride is soon destroyed when teachers are faced with difficult working conditions, a lack of resources, the constant changes of rules, and the adverse judgements of society. As Esteve (1989) points out, society's opinion of the profession has undergone rapid changes. In the inter-war years teachers were thought of as highly educated pillars of society. With the emphasis on social status based on salary in today's society, the values of knowledge, self-sacrifice and vocation have become lost.

> For many parents the fact that someone has chosen to be a teacher is not indicative of a vocation but merely as an 'alibi' for their having been unable to do anything better, that is to say, to do something else which would make more money (p. 12).

Although teachers of pupils with severe learning difficulties, in common with mainstream colleagues, suffer from these judgements, the particular demands made upon them can produce confusion and tension. Society often regards these teachers as having saint-like qualities, of being exceptionally patient, brave and caring; and having the facility to produce miracle cures in children who are not accepted by society at large. The message is complex: teaching itself is not a valued profession but you, as a teacher of 'special' children, are valued. You are highly regarded because your work is unique, but the results of your endeavours are under-valued. It is not surprising, therefore, that many teachers of children with special needs are often in a permanent state of stress! It can be argued that it is usually a continual low-level state; nevertheless, it can cause distress and anxiety if clear social assurance is lacking. On the other hand, it should be realized that low-level stress can become stimulating and energizing and therefore the challenges to help pupils to become acceptable members of an alien society are often exciting and inspiring. There is a risk of some teachers becoming obsessed with aggressive, 'hero innovator' strategies which have little chance of success, and can result in complete disillusionment. The consequent dangers are high levels of stress and the negative consequences.

A number of attempts have been made to define stress in teaching. Dunham (1984) approaches his definition from three disparate positions. The first is the engineering example in which the pressures exerted upon the teacher result in the elastic limits of the capacity to resist being passed. The consequences are psychological or physiological damage, or a combination of the two. These external pressures are more common at specific moments in a teacher's career: probation, re-organization, re-deployment and retirement. The weakness of this definition is that it tends to underestimate the day-to-day demands made upon teachers.

The second is medically-orientated and specifies an unpleasant emotional state characterized by fear, tension, emotional anxiety or exhaustion. Johnstone (1989), in reviewing Dunham's work, states that the danger, implicit in this definition, is that in a search for cures there may be a concentration on the symptoms rather than the causes.

The third example considers the pressures and reactions to stress, together with the coping strategies used by teachers. Stress is only negative in its effects when the pressures are significantly greater than the resources. Dunham's ultimate definition is:

> a process of behavioural, emotional, mental and physical reactions caused by prolonged increasing or new pressures which are significantly greater than coping resources (Dunham, 1984, p. 3).

Defined in this way, stress becomes a dynamic condition open to change as a teacher's resources for coping increase or decline.

These are incisive and useful definitions. In practice, however, teachers and those concerned with the education of pupils with severe learning difficulties need to identify the exact causes of stress. The main factors are:

- challenging behaviours in pupils;
- unsatisfactory relationships with colleagues;
- low morale and adverse political and social responses to their work;
- inadequate working conditions;
- difficulties in matching the teacher's expectations of her own abilities to the responses of her pupils and to the constraints and complexities of the curriculum;
- limited responses from some pupils;
- trauma, including the death of pupils.

Kyriacov's research (1989) into the problems experienced by mainstream teachers and the surveys to which he refers (Dewe, 1986; Freeman, 1987; Laughlin, 1984) appear to confirm these findings, despite differences in context and focus. In mainstream education, for example, pupil indiscipline may pose a problem, whereas in special schools it may appear insignificant compared with deep-seated and disruptive challenging behaviour.

Challenging behaviours

The challenging behaviours displayed by some pupils can be distressing and very difficult to manage. Zarkowska and Clements (1988) estimate that between 50 and 60 per cent of people with learning difficulties present significant behaviour problems. Tantrums and aggression are common in the general population, but bizarre, repetitive, ritualistic and self-injurious behaviours – stripping, soiling, and physical aggression, for example – are more prevalent in people with severe learning difficulties. All of these behaviours can produce stress in a teacher who lacks the knowledge and methods to cope. The results can be demoralization and a serious lack of confidence. Even in the most experienced teacher the constant battle to 'contain' behaviour without the knowledge of particular techniques and approaches can stretch methods of coping beyond acceptable limits. One teacher talked about constantly feeling inept and threatened because she could not control the aggressive outbursts of one pupil. She, on her own admission, was in a state of extreme anxiety and had been absent from school for long periods. In discussions with colleagues, it is apparent that where schools have developed a recognized policy for dealing with inappropriate behaviours, and where teachers are given the opportunity to receive intensive in-service training in behavioural management and therapeutic approaches, coping strategies quickly become part of their personal resources.

Teachers receiving specific in-service training talked positively about the elimination of inappropriate behaviours over a period of time with the help of other colleagues. They viewed their pupils' emotional and behavioural reactions as being extremely annoying and wearing but firmly believed there were opportunities for success.

A pupil displaying extremely challenging behaviours within a class not only taxes the resources of the immediate staff, but of the whole school. As one head teacher reported,

> the behaviour (self-injurious) triggers shock waves throughout the school which are emotionally draining for all staff whether or not they are directly involved.

Problems may occur when staff view the situation as being outside their terms of reference and when the school's organizational structure does not provide support. It is self-evident that if behavioural changes are to be successful long-term, there must be adequate backing and effective communication of information. It may be necessary to re-deploy a member of staff to support the teacher within the class whilst an intensive programme is undertaken. Certainly, collective decisions and plans need to be made and information shared. A whole-school approach offers, on the one hand, greater expertise and the necessary structures for the successful implementation of specific programmes; on the other, crucial social and emotional support for individual teachers.

Relationships with colleagues

The introduction of the National Curriculum has brought about tensions in other ways for teachers of pupils with severe learning difficulties. The major part of the National Curriculum is prescriptive and, on initial examination, bears little resemblance to the curriculum developed through whole-school planning. It is only on closer analysis that teachers can see the connections between their own innovations and the programmes of study for the core subjects. Some teachers have reservations (Staff of Tye Green School, 1991) and feel that the

National Curriculum is irrelevant to the needs of their particular pupils. Others welcome the opportunities to continue the advances made in special education over the past 20 years. Tensions, however, have arisen between teachers, often in the same school, which have resulted in anxiety and hostility. One comment was:

> I feel very isolated in attempting to defend and put into action the National Curriculum. Only the head and the deputy are for it. The rest of the staff pay lipservice to it but are against it secretly. The situation is getting to me.

Local Education Authority (LEA) training and support for the implementation of the National Curriculum has, in many areas of the country, been totally inadequate for teachers of pupils with severe learning difficulties (Tilstone, 1991). Teachers have often been unsure of the LEA's position and, for a policy of entitlement to become a practical reality, more help and support must be available through carefully considered and developed INSET.

The specific problems of the National Curriculum are not the only cause of conflict with colleagues which may cause stress. Teaching pupils with severe learning difficulties involves a multi-professional team, and disagreements can arise when there are struggles between members to gain recognition and power. Despite views to the contrary, Knight and Bowers (1984) suggest that the environments within schools dictate an individualistic pattern of work where members of the team operate independently. In these situations it is easy for conflicts to arise as communication is likely to be poorer and there is less opportunity for mutual problem-solving. Organizational resources are strengthened when staff are given the opportunities to develop skills of communication, cooperation and social support. Freeman and Gray (1989) suggest that one of the most important ways to facilitate coping and to reduce stress is to provide an appropriate caring management structure which enables support systems to operate, by providing time for staff to support each other.

Low morale

A former Permanent Secretary of Education, Sir David Hancock, suggested that 'by far the most serious problems in education are restoring the morale and raising the status of teachers' (*The Guardian*, 1991, p. 18); a view of particular significance in schools for pupils with severe learning difficulties where there is often a conflict between the declared values of a society (which at present makes additional payments to teachers in the form of incentive allowances) and the articulated values of individuals. A councillor, who is a member of an education committee, on visiting a school for pupils with severe learning difficulties commented, 'It is wonderful to see the staff caring for children who are no more than human vegetables'.

Inferences cannot be made from isolated examples, but perhaps the most worrying issue in recent educational history has been the tendency of politicians to ignore some of the needs of pupils with severe learning difficulties as evidenced in the initial National Curriculum documents. Later papers did, however, emphasize the principle of active participation (NCC, 1989). Nevertheless, the conflicting messages teachers were receiving in the early stages have resulted in a general lowering of self-esteem. The research of Kremar and Hofman (1985) has indicated that the undermining of a teacher's professional confidence makes her more vulnerable to burn-out. It is not without significance that local initiatives, outside LEA provisions, have attracted large numbers of anxious teachers whose initial motivation was a desperate need for information and help. For example, monitoring or development groups, in the West Midlands, Manchester, Humberside and East Sussex, have been formed to share concerns and to offer mutual support. Regular meetings provide a forum for debate and opportunities for a welcome exchange of ideas. Teachers from the groups have indicated that the encouragement and assistance made available has enabled them to decrease their anxiety level.

Inadequate working conditions

The closure of many hospital wards and the development of better support services in the community have meant an increase in the number of pupils with profound and multiple learning difficulties in schools (Phillips and Smith, 1979). Unfortunately some of the older buildings still in use were not designed for these children and facilities are often inadequate. The use of specialist equipment and insufficient storage space for wheelchairs can result in cramped conditions. Toilet facilities may be inappropriate and the lack of space for the storage of basic equipment (nappies, bibs and specialized feeding aids) may cause considerable difficulties. The physical strains of dressing, feeding, lifting and changing are often underestimated by senior management. One teacher commented:

> I love my job, but I sometimes get so physically exhausted and mentally frustrated working under difficult environmental conditions that I cannot find the energy to go to work.

It is not, however, only teachers of the profound multiple learning difficulties population who can be disadvantaged by adverse environmental conditions. In one large Authority the special schools were built to a plan which made it necessary to cross the hall in order to get from the administrative block to any classroom. Staff had considerable difficulty in keeping control in these halls during PE, drama, music, and movement lessons with a steady stream of staff and visitors passing through.

It is often assumed that work in special schools generates full collaboration and cooperation but as Knight and Bowers (1984) point out, 'team work' is a glib phrase in special education and difficult to achieve unless it is actively fostered:

> Only when tasks and responsibilities are shared and the act of working together enhances the work that is done can a team be said to have formed (p. 199).

Sharing tasks presents few problems if staff are committed to providing the best possible education for their pupils, but sharing responsibility for each other can be more difficult to achieve. They quote Maslach (1976) who found that stress levels were lower when professionals actively shared personal feelings about their work and when colleagues acknowledged that they had a responsibility for providing mutual support. It is only when the emotional well-being of the staff is fully considered that a school can be regarded as effective (Gray and Freeman, 1987). One head teacher in the south of England has established a multi-faceted support system. Staff are encouraged to share their feelings in an open way and to support each other emotionally. In addition, a weekly clinic is provided by the school nurse to check stress indicators such as blood pressure and weight. Counselling, massage and yoga are also provided.

The mismatch between a teacher's expectations and her pupil's achievements

Pupils with severe learning difficulties are usually involved in sequenced learning programmes which take into account individual development and are ultimately designed as a preparation for life in society. But, as Brennan (1985) points out, it is impossible for schools to present them with every beneficial learning experience and, therefore, staff have to select and prioritize. Consequently, teachers find themselves under constant pressure to review what, and how, they teach, and to be accountable for all their actions to LEAs, school governors, parents and the pupils themselves. Tension can also arise if a teacher has a large number of pupils, or if an individual pupil requires an inordinate amount of her time and attention. She may feel personally responsible for not providing adequate learning experiences for other pupils and may experience serious dissatisfaction.

Teaching children with severe learning difficulties usually involves extra duties and extra responsibilities. To a heavy teaching load and the consequent planning and organization, are added the demands of recording and evaluating, liaison with other professionals and parents, administrative work, and curriculum development, all of which can result in intolerable pressures. As one teacher remarked:

> I have to perform herculean organizational, administrative and public relations tasks, as well as my everyday teaching commitment. I work every evening for at least three hours and find it very difficult to switch off at all. I constantly feel exhausted.

In small special schools most teachers are curriculum coordinators and it is not uncommon for an individual to be responsible for the development of more than one curriculum area. The duties may also include: maintaining and updating stock and resources; leading INSET; writing curriculum documents; monitoring the use of record-keeping systems; liaising with teachers from other schools; working with parents; and promoting community interests. Not only do teachers need training to undertake many aspects of their role (promoting community interests for example) but the problems associated with such a wide range of responsibilities need to be recognized. There will be inevitable conflicts between those aspects of the job which are concerned with the present and those which need long-term planning if stress is to be prevented (Campbell, 1985; Dunham, 1984).

Limited responses from pupils

It is generally recognized that pupils with severe learning difficulties have problems in motivation (Gulliford, 1985). In the main, teachers are prepared to accept that there is a need to foster intrinsic motivation, and consequently develop their own action plan which is concerned with attention, rewards and reinforcement. Throughout, responsive relationships with pupils are essential and will lead to the successful presentation of meaningful activities in the correct context. However, teachers who have worked exclusively with children with multiple learning difficulties over a long period find that the poor motivation of their pupils lowers their own morale. Evans and Ware (1987), in a survey of educational provision in special care units in the south-east of England, found that the lack of feedback from some of the children produced pessimistic attitudes in staff. Many teachers felt that the children could not learn and saw them as different from the remainder of the school population. Experience indicates that it may not be wise for a teacher to stay with the same group for a lengthy period. Two years may be the optimal time and it is usual for head teachers to move staff from class to class at frequent intervals.

With the trend to integrate pupils with profound and multiple learning difficulties into classes for pupils with severe learning difficulties (Carpenter and Lewis, 1989), the stress on individual staff is lessened. However, in appointing a teacher to support such initiatives (as is becoming accepted practice, usually in posts of responsibility) it is important for the school to recognize that the situation can become potentially stressful for three main reasons:

(1) The teacher's job has been defined as dealing solely with pupils who have been labelled for their lack of responsiveness.
(2) The teacher may have to support pupils in some classes where they are not welcome (for a variety of reasons).
(3) Promotion prospects may be jeopardized by holding a specialized teaching post in this discrete area. There may be more opportunities, for example, for a post-holder with responsibility for Science across the curriculum to gain promotion, than for a post-holder for the integration of pupils with profound and multiple learning difficulties.

Therefore, teachers of pupils with profound multiple learning difficulties need not only to be highly trained, but schools need to value and recognize their work and to ensure job satisfaction. Amongst the required factors that Gray and Freeman (1987) identify are appreciation, autonomy, opportunity, good personal relationships, support, influence and specific awards.

Trauma

In special schools, many staff will have experienced the death of a pupil, but in mainstream it is rare. Death is hard to bear at any time, but the death of someone of school age is particularly difficult to cope with and the result is a stressful experience for all staff. There is a general assumption that only the elderly die and consequently the death of a child arouses more complex emotions. In the words of Father John McCullagh, 'When an adult dies, we bury the past. When a child dies, we bury the future and all those might have beens' (1991). Staff may well experience similar emotions to those of bereaved parents, which have been identified as: denial (it can't be true), anger (how could this happen with today's medical advances?), guilt and punishment (why couldn't I do something to prevent it?) and depression (Hill, 1988). The feelings are often intense and can take staff, who pride themselves on their professionalism, completely off-guard.

Teachers also have to face the problem of telling other pupils. It is often assumed that people with severe learning difficulties are unable to understand death and do not need to grieve. Recent research shows that they go through the same stages of grief as others (Crick, 1988; Oswin, 1981) and need similar help and support. Aid is usually available from school staff who may also be experiencing strain and may themselves need professional assistance and counselling. Experience indicates that parents often turn for comfort and reassurance to the staff of the school, who may themselves be seriously disturbed.

Teachers may experience physical symptoms such as sleeplessness, fatigue and loss of appetite after the death of a pupil – all indicators of stress.

Conclusion

It is advisable to consider ways in which present systems can be improved and enhanced in order to offer help and support in all situations.

Many of the difficulties experienced by teachers stem from inadequate and irrelevant national, local and school policies. Morale is ultimately the responsibility of governments and society and, although it is tempting to suggest that increased salaries and additional resources would be a cure for all ills, a full understanding and an exact valuation of work undertaken in schools for pupils with severe learning difficulties depends on good lines of communication with the public at large. Government and local government need to take their responsibilities seriously, along with the teachers' unions, the schools and the teachers themselves. Until teachers of pupils with severe learning difficulties are valued as professionals by all sectors of society, many of the problems outlined above will take their toll.

In-service training can provide solutions to the effects of most of the factors, but too often the training on offer has appeared to be synonymous with 'crisis-management for today's special difficulties' and has not always addressed the real problems: inadequacies in personal and professional development or inefficiencies in management and organization. INSET must be specific. Courses on managing challenging behaviours, on the acquisition of team-teaching skills, on whole-school collaboration on the development and implementation of curriculum change and on specific aspects of the National Curriculum are essential. Industry has been able to develop comparable training aimed at helping supervisors, foremen, middle-managers – why not schools and LEAs? The work undertaken on such courses, however, needs to be extended and enhanced. One possibility is the regular interchange of teachers between classes and between schools. Only then can the individual teacher contextualize her problems, undertake the vital exchange of ideas, and avoid the dangerous feelings of isolation.

The best in-service courses will bring about changes in individuals, but they will also help teachers to understand the nature of change and the ways in which schools can handle the threat of change. Senior management, too, will need to be involved in in-service training as teachers, and as learners. A detailed audit of management policy and practice will lead to increases in efficiency and to the meaningful involvement of all staff. Change is necessary, but forced, ill-understood attempts to bring about changes are counterproductive and inevitably result in stress at all levels. Efficient and valid change ultimately depends on good communications, and the involvement and commitment of all concerned. Teachers who have been given the responsibility of bringing about change need to have their real (not theoretical) roles defined for themselves and their colleagues. Tension will always be present when misunderstanding is unavoidable.

The schools themselves need to be encouraged to take specific initiatives. Senior management can, with benefit to all, involve themselves in the day-to-day running of each classroom. At times, some of the issues dealt with may seem of little significance to the school as a whole, but it is the cumulative effect of the (apparently) most petty problems that push isolated teachers into untenable situations. The value of free and open discussions has already been stressed, but the importance of ensuring that these take place regularly and that the time devoted to them is adequate should not be ignored. Teachers demonstrate imagination and initiative in providing attractive environments, on a shoe-string, for their pupils, but find difficulties in bringing about changes in the functional characteristics of a school. Teachers are also managers (of the classroom environment and resources) and it pays in terms of efficiency and morale to ensure that their views and ideas are noted.

Finally, however, there must be support systems for those who are unable to cope with the pressures. Colleagues may provide sympathetic understanding, but often a professional response is needed. There are good models of practice which include the availability of medical check ups and skilled counselling but, in the present climate of change, initiatives and decisions will have to come from within the schools themselves. It is these (apparently) minor services which contribute to the general good, and ensure the efficient use of all resources and the effective education of all children.

References

Brennan, W. K. (1985) *Curriculum for Special Needs*. Milton Keynes: Open University Press.

Carpenter, B. and Lewis, A. (1989) 'Searching for solutions: Approaches to planning the curriculum for the integration of SLD and PMLD children', in Baker, D. and Bovair, K. (Eds) *Making the Special Schools Ordinary Volume 1*. London: Falmer Press.

Campbell, R. J. (1985) *Developing the Primary School Curriculum*. Sussex: Holt, Rinehart & Winston.

Crick, L. (1988) 'Facing grief', *Nursing Times*, 84, 28, pp. 61–3.

Dewe, P. J. (1986) 'An investigation into the causes and consequences of teacher stress', *New Zealand Journal of Educational Studies*, 21, pp. 145–57.

Dunham, J. (1984) *Stress in Teaching*. Beckenham: Croom Helm.

Esteve, J. (1989) 'Teacher burnout and teacher stress', in Cole, M. and Walker, S. (Eds) *Teaching and Stress*. Milton Keynes: Open University Press.

Evans, P. and Ware, J. (1987) *'Special Care' Provision: The Education of Children with Profound and Multiple Learning Difficulties*. Windsor: NFER-Nelson.

Freeman, A. (1987) 'Pastoral care and teacher stress', *Pastoral Care in Education*, 5, pp. 22–8.

Freeman, A. and Gray, H. (1989) *Organising Special Educational Needs – A Critical Approach*. London: Paul Chapman.

Gray, H. and Freeman, A. (1987) *Teaching without Stress*. London: Paul Chapman.

The Guardian (1991) Comment. 18 April, p. 18.

142

Gulliford, R. (1985) *Teaching Children with Learning Difficulties*. Windsor: NFER-Nelson.

Hargreaves, A. and Woods, D. (Eds) (1984) *Classrooms and Staffrooms. The Sociology of Teachers Teaching*. Milton Keynes: Open University Press.

Hill, L. (1988) 'Coping', *Research Trust for Metabolic Diseases in Children: News*, 8, 2, pp. 3–5.

Johnstone, M. (1989) *Stress in Teaching. An Overview of Research*. Midlothian: The Scottish Council for Research in Education.

Knight, R. and Bowers, T. (1984) 'Developing effective teams', in Bowers, T. (Ed.) *Management and the Special School*. London: Croom Helm.

Kremer, L. and Hofman, J.E. (1985) 'Teacher's professional identity and burnout', *Research in Education*, 34, pp. 89–95.

Kyriacov, C. (1989) 'The nature and prevalence of teacher stress', in Cole, M. and Walker, S. (Eds) *Teaching and Stress*. Milton Keynes: Open University Press.

Laughlin, A. (1984) 'Teacher stress in an Australian setting: The role of the biographical mediators', *Educational Studies*, 10, pp. 7–22.

McCullagh, J. (1991) *Prayer for the Day*, 16 May, BBC Radio 4.

Maslach, C. (1976) 'Burn-out', *Human Behaviour*, 5, pp. 76–8.

Oswin, M. (1981) *Bereavement and Mentally Handicapped People: A Discussion Paper*. London: Kings Fund.

National Curriculum Council (1989) *Circular No. 5: Implementing the National Curriculum – Participation by Pupils with Special Educational Needs*. York: NCC.

Phillips, C. J. and Smith, B. (Eds) (1979) *Severely Educationally Handicapped Children (Birmingham 1973–5) Vol 3*. Birmingham: Centre for Child Study, University of Birmingham.

Staff of Tye Green School (1991) 'Broad, balanced . . . and relevant?', *Special Children*, 44, January, pp. 11–13.

Tilstone, C. (1991) 'Teacher education: The changing focus', in Ashdown, R., Carpenter, B. and Bovair, K. (Eds) *The Curriculum Challenge*. London: Falmer Press.

Zarkowska, E. and Clements, J. (1988) *Problem Behaviour in People with Severe Learning Difficulties*. London: Croom Helm.

PART THREE

CHAPTER 11

Changing Attitudes

Barry Carpenter, Julie Moore and Sylvia Lindoe

Shared learning: the practice of integration. *Barry Carpenter*

The integration debate has widely influenced all aspects of special education and schools for children with severe learning difficulties have found it necessary to undertake a close examination of their educational philosophy in the light of trends towards the greater integration of their children. The 'egalitarian approach' suggested by Tomlinson (1982) has had to be considered alongside the phases of integration (locational, social and functional) identified by the Warnock Report (DES, 1978), which provides a framework for educational modes of integration. But what is the intended outcome of these processes? Schools are ideal sponsoring bodies for initiatives in integration but how valuable are these initiatives if, in post-school life, segregation and suspicion about the 'handicapped' continue?

As the process of normalization is widely advocated for people with learning difficulties to enable them to live as full members of their local communities, a societal level of integration is desirable to prepare children in special and mainstream settings for citizenship. In May 1990, the Council and Ministers of Education of the European Community passed a resolution which acknowledged that full integration into the system of mainstream education should be considered as the first option in all appropriate cases for children and young people with disabilities, and that all educational establishments should be in a position to respond to their needs. In passing this resolution the Council specifically stated that the work of special schools and centres for children and young people with disabilities should be seen as complementary to the work of the ordinary education system.

Blythe School in Warwickshire is one of the many schools that have accepted the challenge. Over the past eight years it has developed extensive integration links across all phases of education, not only with schools in the direct locality but with others from within its rural catchment area. (A detailed record of these projects is provided in the Note at the end of this chapter).

The appointment of an Integration Support Teacher greatly enhanced the initial links with other schools. Within Blythe School itself staff ensured that children with profound and multiple learning difficulties did not endure a 'double segregation' (Ouvry, 1987) by remaining solely within a 'special care' unit. Gradually, integration programmes have been extended to the previously 'segregated' children with profound and multiple learning difficulties and who are now educated alongside their peers with severe learning difficulties. The ultimate goal was reached with the assimilation into the Further Education Department (16–19-year-olds) of students with profound and multiple learning difficulties, enabling them to gain access to colleges of further education and the extensive, community-based leisure facilities. It could be argued, however, that despite these successes, the pupils would have gained even greater benefits if the integration schemes had been introduced in their early years.

Early intervention, early integration

A number of intervention strategies for children with special educational needs offer a positive means of minimizing handicaps and facilitating support for parents, the most notable of which is the Portage Project (Bluma *et al.*, 1976). A Home Liaison Playgroup was established at Blythe School in recognition of the desirability of early intervention and parental support, and over the years it gradually developed into a Community Playgroup. Thus early intervention initiated early integration. The target group for the Community Playgroup included children with special needs who had been part of the Home Liaison Playgroup plus 20 local pre-school children of two years of age and above. The parents of all children were also invited to the weekly meetings.

Moyles (1989) gives some excellent examples of play for children with special educational needs and argues that play can offer a basis for children to explore situations that they may meet in their everyday lives. Thus, as a facilitator and a motivator, it may provide a sound foundation for integration. She also suggests that play can be used as a therapy for disturbed or perturbed children. It is essential to realize that some children in mainstream schools may find it disturbing to be confronted with a child with a significant disability and that children need to be given space and time to come to terms with their feelings and responses. Play offers pupils a vehicle for discovering about each other; it offers teachers a vehicle for planning to meet individual needs.

Involving parents

Parents were familiar with the principles underlying the projects developed from Blythe School and, in giving their whole-hearted support, proved that they have a major contribution to make to the development of integration. It had been assumed by staff that some of the parents of mainstream children would have reservations about the benefits to their own children but in the event they were enthusiastic and confirmed the conclusions of Lewis (1991) who cites the example of an integration project when a parent complained that her own child was not taking part.

The project also involved the establishment of a parents' centre, linked to the Integrated Nursery, which provided a venue for informal meetings, a reference library, and a toy-lending library. The consequent opportunities for discussion and the interchange of ideas led to two important developments. The parents of mainstream children became increasingly realistic in their expectation of, and more positive in their approach to, children with special needs; a vital step as the positive responses of a parent are powerful factors in the shaping of a young child's attitudes to disability.

Encouraging citizenship

Children from mainstream schools often show a natural curiosity about children with severe learning difficulties and may question the term 'Down's syndrome' or the fact that they have overheard an adult describing their friend as 'brain damaged'. In the projects cited by Lewis and Carpenter (1990) it is interesting to note that the initial focus of these questions is on the child, and not on the handicap. During preparatory work for the project, therefore, preliminary discussions used videos and stories about children with severe learning difficulties. The inappropriateness of treating children with severe learning difficulties as helpless babies was emphasized throughout, and Makaton Signs, learned at an early stage by mainstream children, were revised and supplemented. Positive attitudes towards disability are crucial if integration projects are to have a sustained effect on the personal and social development of all children. Appropriate resources too are essential for an adequate exploration of a range of disability issues. In a lecture, Rix (1990) considered that a 'lack of understanding and acceptance on the part of teachers, other pupils and their parents have all contributed to the slow progress of integration'.

Le Metais (1988), reviewing a range of integration practices throughout Europe, focused upon physical and sensory handicaps and found that many countries had policies based on holistic principles, dealing with all special educational needs. To whatever degree each country had achieved the integration of pupils with severe learning difficulties, there was a general lack of specific attention to the development of positive attitudes in mainstream children towards their peers with disabilities. It is therefore vital that schools accept responsibility for this task; if they do not, how can they expect society at large to take its own obligations seriously?

It is encouraging to realize that in the context of *The Whole Curriculum* (NCC, 1990), citizenship is one of the five cross-curricular themes. The Education Reform Act itself (DES, 1988) places a statutory responsibility upon schools to provide a broad and balanced curriculum which prepares pupils for the opportunities, responsibilities and experiences of adult life. HMI (1990) similarly emphasizes that it is essential for the curriculum to serve the child by the promotion of personal development and preparation for adult life. Integration can be a prime facilitator for citizenship and for many of the reasons mentioned above, it offers opportunities for attitudinal developments that are vital to the total education of our future citizens. We must, therefore, ask what can be the basis for meaningful shared learning between our children? What will promote, guide and stimulate the development of true citizenship?

Sharing the curriculum

Through careful negotiation, a range of integration projects was generated for the Blythe School pupils to take place either in mainstream schools or at times in the special school itself. As the choice of curriculum area is crucial to the success of any integration project, Drama, Home Economics, Music, Mathematics, PE and Arts have been explored and careful thought needs to be given to ways in which these areas relate to the National Curriculum. The emphasis, however, in any integration programme must be on the opportunities that it provides for shared learning experiences between children of all abilities and in which every pupil is an active participant. It is essential to avoid situations in which children with special educational needs become 'peripheral participants'. In addition, the significance of learning gains, and ways in which they can make a major contribution to a child's development, must be considered during planning.

A key construct of the National Curriculum is differentiation. King (1990) argues that 'differentiation is about meeting the needs of all learners and requires a concern with the pupil, the task and the learning context' (p. 22). All learners are different and all teaching needs to be differentiated and it is through the strength of differentiation that children with severe learning difficulties will be given access to the National Curriculum, and that continuity and progression will be ensured. Similarly, it is through differentiation that children in integrated settings will be given access to meaningful curriculum experiences.

The National Curriculum offers a common curriculum nucleus from which the learning experiences of children can be planned, and enhances the curriculum dialogue between teachers in each phase of education. A recurrent question from mainstream teachers involved in integration projects is 'What do you do at your school?'. The confident response should be:

> The curriculum is the same, but the methodology and resources may be different in order to facilitate the level and quality of differentiation demanded by children with severe learning difficulties

Archer (1989) records the use of National Curriculum statements of attainment to guide curricular decisions across special and ordinary schools, an approach which offers potentially improved negotiation for integration support teachers. They are then able to define the experience required from a common curriculum starting point. For example, an integration support teacher may suggest to a school that a child needs Science at level 3. From this broad statement teachers can explore together what is required within leve 3, which attainment targets are relevant, and how they are to be delivered.

Lewis (1991) gives an example of how children of different abilities can work effectively on a common task within the National Curriculum. If, for example, children working in pairs are making 'three dimensional' shapes from 'two dimensional' card or plastic, one child could be required to sort the shapes by colour (Science AT15 level 1) or by shape (Mathematics AT10 level 1), and the other child could build pyramids or cubes (Mathematics AT10 level 4).

'Mini-beasts' has been a popular project in primary and special schools. Using a sensory garden area in a special school, children with severe learning difficulties were able to share the exploration, investigation and excitement with their mainstream infant peers. Working in this way, they touched upon a range of Science Attainment Targets (AT1 level 1, AT2 levels 1, 2, and 3, AT3 levels 1 and 2). The activities outlined by Howe (1991) indicate how, through the whole of the National Curriculum Science attainment targets, a variety of topics can be generated which are ideal potential material for shared learning between all children. Longhorn (1991) imaginatively illuminates a range of sensory approaches to Science which would enable children with profound and multiple learning difficulties to share in learning with their peers.

Recently, a group of 8-year-olds in a mainstream first school considered the *Tactile Stories* (Fuller, 1990) and planned a Technology project. They identified the need for children with profound and multiple learning difficulties to enjoy a story that was appropriate to their development at level AT1. They then generated their own story design for which each component could be linked to a tactile experience and planned and made their stories using a variety of materials. They collected fabrics and selected the appropriate glues to stick them to card; they chose different smells to link into aspects of the story (AT3); they incorporated information technology into their work by word-processing their story (AT5). The evaluation (AT4) came in the delivery of the story to a group of young children with profound and multiple learning difficulties. The 8-year-olds supported each child physically, to touch, to smell and to listen to all aspects of the story that they had created. There were shouts of glee from all children as they discovered joy in sharing. A week later the project was repeated when the children with profound and multiple learning difficulties actually took part in the composition of the story. The mainstream group of children had identified something of interest to the children with profound and multiple learning difficulties and had proceeded to cut and to paste and to make their story with the other children as partial participants in the technological process (Carpenter, 1990; Marsh, 1988). The mainstream children in this setting were both facilitators and supporters of the learning.

Throughout many of the above examples, considerable linguistic demands are made on all children. Group work and collaborative approaches mean that each child has to reconcile his linguistic talents and abilities with those of his peer group (Lewis and Carpenter, 1990). This in itself poses opportunities within the context of the English National Curriculum (Carpenter, 1991, in press) and demonstrates how augmentative approaches using signs and symbols will be necessary to enhance the programme of study in English for children with severe learning difficulties. Such approaches could run alongside the experiences being offered to mainstream children. This is the essence of differentiation. The mode of delivery may be different, but the children learn, and learn effectively.

The pattern of integration activities outlined above reflects the development from tentative beginnings towards a commitment to maximizing the benefits of integrated or segregated settings. The types of partial integration described offer children with severe learning difficulties contact with mainstream children in the immediate neighbourhood. Practice at Blythe School has demonstrated ways in which the curriculum can facilitate shared learning. The opportunities offered must be used to standardize curriculum terminology, to deepen current understanding of the learning experiences of all children and to prepare, through a common curriculum, all children for meaningful citizenship.

Special schools exist owing to historical circumstances, but they do not have the right to do so. Dessent (1987) reminds us that they still remain as a result of the limitations of mainstream schools in providing for the different abilities of all pupils. The practice of segregated special education, although deeply ingrained, is slowly being eroded. The pupils at the extreme end of a special needs continuum no longer pose such a threat to the mainstream education system, although there is a lack of reliable national statistics on how many pupils with severe learning difficulties are being educated full-time in mainstream schools.

The developments made to integrate pupils have been mainly due to the efforts of staff from special schools (Mittler and Farrell, 1987) and mainstream schools have rarely made the initial approach. A National

Foundation for Educational Research survey in 1987 showed that a greater proportion of schools for pupils with severe learning difficulties had developed links with other kinds of special schools (Jowett *et al.*, 1988). 'Links' can be interpreted in many different ways: from children mixing together in social situations, to groups of pupils from both schools being taught together, to individual special school pupils being educated in mainstream schools (CSIE, 1985; North West Mental Handicap Development Team, 1989).

The majority of schools for pupils with severe learning difficulties have established two models of integration: the first involves the movement of classes, where pupils, teachers and resources go into mainstream and special schools as a group; the second arranges for children to go, with varying degrees of support from the special school, to spend time in the mainstream school. Care has to be taken in both cases to ensure that pupils are encouraged to interact. Special schools have a duty to hasten the changes of attitude by the community to pupils with severe learning difficulties. Structured attitude change needs to be implemented at all levels.

The following section, in which Julie Moore (formerly head teacher at Nethersole's School) described an early integration project with Blythe School, highlights the necessity for careful planning in order to achieve effective interaction. The work described is typical of many small-scale projects throughout the country, the majority of which are not documented or evaluated.

Integration: the mainstream perspective. *Julie Moore*

Nethersole's Church of England First School is seven miles from Blythe School. Preliminary meetings between the head teachers formulated realistic aims for the promotion of relationships between pupils and considered ways of helping mainstream pupils to develop positive attitudes toward their peers with severe learning difficulties.

The aims for the pupils of both schools were essentially complementary. For the Nethersole's school pupils they were designed to:

- provide opportunities to meet and work with children who have multiple learning difficulties;
- encourage interaction with the special school pupils through play and

communication;

- acquire insights into the needs of children with severe learning difficulties;
- develop an awareness of the problems experienced by children with severe learning difficulties in school, at home and in their community;
- plan ways in which these children can be supported and helped;
- cultivate a tolerant attitude to abnormal behaviour;
- develop an understanding of the social unacceptability of certain behaviours;
- provide opportunities to help special school children in the acquisition of fine and gross motor skills.

The pupils from Blythe School would be given opportunities to:

- mix and interact with their mainstream peers;
- develop a range of strategies in order to form relationships through all forms of communication.

The aims of the project were concerned primarily with attitudes and reflect adult perceptions which tend to be imposed upon the children. In practice, however, children from the two schools shared the learning experiences. Attitudinal developments stemmed from the shared curriculum and the explicit focus anticipated by mainstream staff was not required.

The fortnightly interaction sessions were based in the mainstream school and focused on creative activities, in order to provide opportunities for the development and practice of language and communication skills. In the initial stage, 10 Nethersole's children (of a similar age to the Blythe children) were chosen on the basis of good communication skills and for their friendly, outgoing and positive attitudes.

At the end of the first year of the project all Nethersole's children were given an opportunity to be involved and names were chosen at random. Careful preparation of the mainstream pupils was seen as essential and a video of the Blythe children taking part in a PE session was shown. The consequent wide-ranging discussion centred on the physical disabilities of some of the Blythe children, 'How do they get changed for PE?', 'Is it hard for them?'. The children also commented on the high quality of the PE equipment at Blythe School and were envious of the opportunities for large-apparatus work. They also listened to a story about a boy with a disability. This introductory session focused on what the Blythe children could do, and at no time was the word 'handicapped' used by either staff or the children themselves.

There were subsequent meetings between the teachers involved and it was agreed that the joint creative activities (within the project) would also be linked to work in progress. It was anticipated that, as children would be given the opportunities within the shared sessions to follow their own interests, some pooling of resources would be necessary. This flexibility enabled children from both schools to plan cross-curricular activities spanning Maths and Science. The negotiation of their own learning experiences was already familiar to pupils from Nethersole's School, but although it was a new experience for the Blythe pupils, it is now firmly established as part of the curriculum.

The class teachers agreed to alternate the coordination of each session, using a common framework which involved an introductory discussion on the possibilities of the activities offered; work in pairs or small groups; and a plenary session. Time was also set aside for staff to plan, discuss and evaluate as a group, and indicators of the success of the collaboration were the lengthy telephone conversations following reflections upon the work in progress! A termly after-school meeting was programmed at which discussions were always frank and open.

During the second year of the project, Warwickshire LEA appointed integration support teachers to the staff of all special schools and the appointment at Blythe made liaison and organization between both schools much easier. The role of the support teacher was to plan, organize and manage all integration projects, and regular meetings between the staff involved in each scheme were arranged. In addition, half-termly evaluation meetings were held which ensured that each project had a unified structure of planning, implementation and evaluation.

The governors of both schools were kept informed of developments and proved very supportive. Parents of mainstream children commented that their children talked a great deal about the Blythe children but not about their handicaps. Nethersole's School was already involved in a number of projects which brought diverse groups of children into the building (including children from ethnic minorities) and Blythe children were not perceived as different.

Detailed observations of the behaviour of the Nethersole's children during the school year showed four distinct phases of development. The first was characterized by their high level of interaction with the Blythe staff which could be interpreted as a response to the novelty of having new adults in the classroom, eager to communicate with the children, who provided a 'safe' relationship. The second phase was marked by the frequent withdrawal by Nethersole's children from social contact and the open staring at individual children from Blythe school. (The need for 'sanctioned staring' is discussed later in this chapter.) Pupils entered a third phase in the second term of the project as Nethersole's children attempted to communicate through the use of gesture, and Makaton signing was discovered to be a stimulating and novel method of communication from which they received a high level of response. The fourth stage in the interaction process began with an unexpected emphasis on verbal communication as the mainstream pupils attempted to initiate complicated dialogues.

It became apparent, at the end of the year, that the responses of the Nethersole's children had undergone radical changes. They had begun to demonstrate an increasing sensitivity to, and an understanding of, the needs of children with severe learning difficulties. One Nethersole's boy, for example, who had initially been reticent with the Blythe children was, by the end of the first year, defending the behaviour of a particular pupil to a visitor by explaining 'he can do it really'. The Blythe children also derived great benefit from the project and became increasingly confident in communicating with the First School children. Their teachers noted that their social skills had improved and that they had more confidence when communicating with visitors. The improvements are detailed in the literature (see the Notes at the end of this chapter).

Finally, the parents of all the children involved were invited to an evening meeting in order to discuss their perceptions of the project and to provide additional information for its evaluation.

The partial integration of pupils with support

As an extension of the initial project it was decided to integrate two children from Blythe School for one whole day per week with the help of the integration support teacher. The parents were willing and happy to allow their children to attend Nethersole's school on a weekly basis, but expressed a wish that their children should remain on the roll of Blythe School. Joy, aged 5, and David, aged 7, were integrated into the reception unit consisting of two classes of 32 children each. Both classes provide a range of ongoing activities from which the children are free to choose. Teachers and helpers work with them, either individually or in small groups, and their daily experiences are carefully monitored and recorded. This flexible situation suited the needs of Joy and David and they were able to choose specific activities which interested them and to experience more specific teaching in a range of skills.

Integration: planned interaction — the first steps. *Sylvia Lindoe*

Introduction

The greatest single challenge facing those involved with young people is to ensure that they are helped to participate fully in the life of the community. Dewey (1897) suggested that:

> The school is primarily a social institution. Education being a social process, the school is simply that form of community life in which all those agencies are conc ntrated that will be most effective in bringing the child to share in the inherited resources of the race, and use his powers to social ends (p. 23).

Dewey's beliefs would appear to be self-evident, but it took over three-quarters of a century for them to be generally accepted in Britain, as children with severe learning difficulties did not become the responsibility of educationalists until 1971. The debate on where, within the education system, these children should be placed continues. The idea that all children, whatever their needs, must be educated together and share resources is attractive as it would appear to guarantee full integration. In practice, however, a shared campus or building does not necessarily lead to full and meaningful participation in the life of the school.

Nevertheless, it has become increasingly obvious that the facilities provided in many special schools, particularly those with low rolls and a wide age-range, do not adequately meet all the needs of their pupils. It is often impossible to ensure that every child is in his peer group, with consequent serious constraints on opportunities for social development. Limited equipment and buildings, perhaps considered progressive when planned, often inhibit the development of a relevant whole-school curriculum and it has become essential to develop projects which make mainstream opportunities available to pupils with severe learning difficulties.

In initiating a programme of integration, the disparate expectations and values of all concerned should be recognized as positive resources and not be allowed to become a barrier to genuine interaction. Good ideas, good intentions and enthusiasm must be translated into reality.

The primary aim will always be to ensure that people with disabilities are helped and encouraged to move from a purely passive role to becoming full and active participants in all aspects of the life of the community.

The key to success lies in careful and detailed planning. Arrangements for accommodation, transport and meetings may prove relatively easy to make. The greater challenge is to ensure that the programme is designed to focus on interactions between two groups of pupils which will result in the development of friendships. Unless interactions and friendships are considered to be the main priority, pupils with severe learning difficulties may be totally isolated outside the formal classroom provision. It is in these situations that the greatest pull towards friendship groups is experienced in the absence of the kinds of structures found in the classroom. Full and detailed consideration must therefore be given to the potential problems.

Sandler and Robinson (1981) stress that attitudes towards people with severe learning difficulties need to be improved if programmes of de-institutionalization are to succeed, and that schools themselves have the potential to provide the starting point. The available literature is extensive, but the following sources proved particularly relevant. McConkey and McCormack (1983) indicate practical ways of changing community attitudes to disability, and their thinking has been influential. They stress that young people with severe learning difficulties should have equal status with their mainstream peers and that they should not be seen as the recipients of help. They also suggest that informal and casual contacts are rarely fruitful and that planned opportunities for regular meetings and collaborative work are essential. Donaldson (1980) similarly emphasizes the importance of detailed planning. Baldwin and Wells (1979) highlight the need for active involvement and periods of discussion and reflection as a means of effective learning. They also argue that all pupils need to be involved at all stages: in decision-making, planning, organization and management.

Langer et al. (1976) note that non-disabled persons often avoid those with handicaps owing to the discomfort resulting from the conflict between a desire to stare and a desire to adhere to the cultural norms against staring. They found that staring increased when unobserved and was therefore sanctioned; the reverse occurred when an observer was present. The avoidance of physical contact at an initial meeting can be reduced by previously giving the subjects opportunities to observe their disabled partners. The use of video-recordings is an effective method of sanctioned staring. Empathy can also be an important factor in changing attitudes. Clore and Jeffray (1972) suggest that regular meetings with people with disabilities can bring about radical changes in attitudes and a reduction in avoidance. The new perspectives are developed either by significantly reducing discomfort, unease or uncertainty on the part of the non-disabled person or by presenting enough information to contradict the previously held stereotypes.

The programme outlined below, which was developed jointly by a comprehensive and a special school, drew on many of the ideas discussed above.

The programme

Preliminary discussions were held with the staff of the two schools in the Autumn term, using Community Attitudes to Retarded Adults (CARA) (McConkey *et al.*, 1983a) materials, in order to consider the relevance of the methods used to establish links between primary schools and to identify opportunities for the forging of connections with comprehensive schools (McConkey *et al.*, 1983b). Further discussions were then arranged between senior staff from the comprehensive and the special school, and the LEA adviser for special education. It was decided to co-opt the school's coordinator for special needs and the head of third year into the team, and that a module should be developed as part of a third-year tutor group's Personal and Social Education. A need for in-service work with mainstream staff was recognized. Issues of particular interest were identified from a preliminary questionnaire, on which a training session was based during the Spring term.

The pupils' programme

A questionnaire (also based on CARA) was prepared for 25 pupils in the mainstream school and was administered at the end of the Spring term. The first section focused on the pupils' knowledge of special schools and on contacts previously made with people with disabilities. Only two pupils had had any direct contact with the disabled but seven stated that they had seen people with disabilities in television programmes. Pupils were also asked about the causes of 'mental handicap' (a term used as it was felt to be more generally understood than 'severe learning difficulties'), the lives that people with a mental handicap might lead and their own feelings about, and responses to, people with disabilities. There was little evidence to suggest that pupils had considered the causes of handicap but some anecdotal examples of life styles were given. It was generally agreed that sorrow would be the main emotional response but only four were prepared to have more contact with people with a mental handicap.

In the following session, at the beginning of the Summer term, the mainstream pupils met the project team (which included in-service students from the University) and discussed the completed questionnaire in small groups. Slides were also shown of pupils from special schools successfully completing difficult tasks.

The pupils from the special school had, by this time, been introduced to the project through working discussions and had made a video of themselves in practical situations talking about their lives and their leisure activities. The completed video was used during the third session in the mainstream school and some pupils expressed an interest in meeting pupils from the special school. Although eventually 17 of the 20 were keen to be involved in regular meetings, it was concluded that it would be more appropriate if six of them initially met six special school pupils and that feedback to the rest of the group would take place during tutorial periods.

The mainstream pupils then planned a programme for the first half-day visit by the pupils from the special school. They undertook arrangements, including negotiations for rooms and the sending out of invitations to their visitors. During the following five weeks the two groups met for half a day per week. Sessions within a 'social framework', included cookery, snooker (and other 'club' activities), swimming, a visit to a ten-pin bowling alley and a sports afternoon. In week three of the shared programme the special school pupils invited the mainstream pupils back and opportunities were provided for them to meet other young people.

By the end of the project, ten of the mainstream pupils had been directly involved. They had all found the project worthwhile and their answers to a second questionnaire indicated that there had been a shift in attitude, although those who had had direct contact were noticeably more positive and enthusiastic. The view most frequently expressed was that the experience had reduced their fear of people with a mental handicap.

This limited project suggests that it is possible to develop practical strategies for worthwhile contacts between mainstream pupils and pupils with severe learning difficulties. Success is clearly dependent upon careful planning at each stage, with interaction between pupils as the key objective.

Despite the many challenges of the Education Reform Act for all schools, one of the main tasks for schools for pupils with severe learning difficulties must be to equip young people to gain access to their communities. Projects of this kind can be a major method of ensuring participation and understanding.

Conclusion

Many pupils with severe learning difficulties are being educated full-time in mainstream schools with varying degrees of support, particularly at primary level. The National Curriculum offers a positive step towards integration, as it provides mainstream and special schools with a common terminology. Educationalists now, more than ever before, have to work from the starting point of pupil entitlement and their need to justify any deviations from it. Local Management of Schools poses a challenge. There has been considerable anxiety about open enrolment, the publication of results, and the likely effect on the ways in which pupils with special educational needs are welcomed into mainstream schools. However Circular 7/91 (DES, 1991) is encouraging in so far as it provides the opportunity for the funding of outreach to be built into the formula for both mainstream and special schools. Positive attitudes are crucial. Some LEAs, where strong integration policies already exist, have found innovative ways of ensuring that the momentum of integration is maintained (O'Grady, 1991).

There is evidence to suggest that pupils with severe learning difficulties in mainstream schools benefit socially (Mittler and Farrell, 1987; Sebba, 1983) and often academically, particularly at the nursery and infant stage (Lindsay and Desforges, 1986) in fully integrated settings. It is not, however, the child alone who determines success but his interaction with the environment and the adults and children within it (Bennett and Cass, 1989). The carefully planned interaction schemes described above must continue to be an important part of the special schools' curriculum if Fraser's third handicapping factor, that of society's attitudes, is to be addressed (Fraser, 1984).

If pupils with severe learning difficulties are to be prepared for society, society must be prepared for them.

Notes

The following provide a detailed record of the Blythe School project.

Carpenter, B. (1987) 'Curriculum planning for children with profound and multiple learning difficulties', *Early Child Development and Care*, 28, 2, pp. 149–62.

Carpenter, B. (1990) 'The curriculum for children with profound and multiple learning difficulties: current issues', *Australasian Journal of Special Education*, 13, 2, pp. 20–37.

Carpenter, B. and Carpenter, S. A. (1989) 'The Blythe Home-Liaison Playgroup: An example of early intervention for children with special education needs', *Early Child Development and Care*, 53, pp. 13–21.

Carpenter, B. and Cobb, M. (1990) 'Learning together: Practice in an integrated nursery setting', in Jones, N. (Ed.) *Special Needs Review: Volume 3*. London: Falmer Press.

Carpenter, B. and Lewis, A. (1989) 'Searching for solutions: Approaches to planning the curriculum for integration of children with SLD and PMLD children', in Baker, D. and Bovair, K. (Eds) *Making the Special School Ordinary*? London: Falmer Press.

Carpenter, B., Lewis, A. and Moore, J. (1986) 'Integration: A project involving children with severe learning difficulties and First School Children', *Mental Handicap*, 14, 4, pp. 152–7.

Carpenter, B., Fathers, J., Lewis, A. and Privett, R. (1988) 'Integration. The Coleshill experience', *British Journal of Special Education*, 15, 3, pp. 119–21.

Moore, J., Carpenter, B. and Lewis, A. (1987) ' "He can do it really" – integration in a First School', *Education 3–13*, 15, 2, pp. 37–43.

Tompkins, A. and Carpenter, B. (1990) 'A post-16 education for students with profound and multiple learning difficulties', *Mental Handicap*, 18, pp. 105–8.

References

Archer, M. (1989) 'Targetting change', *Special Children*, 33, pp. 14–15.

Baldwin, J. and Wells, H. (1979) *Active Tutorial Work Books 1–5*. Oxford: Blackwell.

Bennett, N. and Cass, A. (1989) *From Special to Ordinary Schools. Case Studies in Integration*. London: Cassell.

Bluma, S., Shearer, M., Frohman, A. and Hilliard, J. (1976) *Portage Guide to Early Education Manual*. Wisconsin: CESA.

Carpenter, B. (1990) 'The curriculum for children with profound and multiple learning difficulties: current issues', *Australasian Journal of Special Education*, 13, 2, pp. 20–37.

Carpenter, B. (1991, in press) 'Unlocking the door: Access to English in the National Curriculum', in Smith, B. (Ed.) *Interactive Approaches to the Core Subjects*. Bristol: Lame Duck.

162

Centre for Studies on Integration in Education (1985) *Transferring Good Practice. Factsheet.* London: NCSE.

Clore, J. and Jeffray, J. (1972) 'Emotional role playing, attitude change and attraction toward a disabled person', *Journal of Personality and Social Psychology*, 23, pp. 105–11.

Department of Education and Science (1978) *Special Educational Needs: Report of the Committee of Enquiry into the Education of Handicapped Children and Young People* (The Warnock Report). London: HMSO.

Department of Education and Science (1988) *The Education Reform Act.* London: HMSO.

Department of Education and Science (1990) *Education Observed. Special Needs Issues. A Survey by HMI.* London: HMSO. '

Department of Education and Science (1991) *Local Management of Schools: Further Guidance*, Circular 7/91. London: HMSO.

Dessent, T. (1987) *Making the Ordinary School Special.* London: Falmer Press.

Dewey, J. (1897) in Bantock, G. H. (1973) *Education In An Industrial Society.* London: John Dickens.

Donaldson, J. (1980) 'Changing attitudes towards handicapped persons: A review and analysis of research', *Exceptional Children*, 46, 7, pp. 504–14.

Fraser, B. (1984) *Society, Schools and Handicap.* Stratford: NCSE.

Fuller, C. (1990) *Tactile Stories.* London: Resources of Learning Difficulties: The Consortium.

Howe, L. (1991) 'Approaches to science', in Ashdown, R., Carpenter, B. and Bovair, K. (Eds) *The Curriculum Challenge.* London: Falmer Press.

Jowett, S., Hegarty, S. and Moses, D. (1988) *Joining Forces: A Study of Links between Special and Ordinary Schools.* Windsor: NFER-Nelson.

King, V. (1990) 'Differentiation is the key', *Language and Learning*, 3, pp. 22–4.

Langer, E. J., Fisher, S., Taylor, S. E. and Chanowitz, B. (1976) 'Stigma, staring and discomfort: A novel stimulus hypothesis', *Journal of Experimental Social Psychology*, 12, pp. 451–63.

Le Metais, J. (1988) *Educational Provision for Pupils with Physical Handicaps in the European Community.* Slough: Epic Europe/NFER.

Lewis, A. (1991) 'Entitled to learn together?', in Ashdown, R., Carpenter, B. and Bovair, K. (Eds) *The Curriculum Challenge.* London: Falmer Press.

Lewis, A. and Carpenter, B. (1990) 'Discourse in an integrated school setting, between six and seven-year old non-handicapped children and peers with severe learning difficulties', in Frazer, W. I. (Ed.) *Key Issues in Mental Retardation Research.* London: Routledge.

Lindsay, G. and Desforges, M. (1986) 'Integrated nurseries for children with SEN', *British Journal of Special Education*, 13, 2, pp. 63–6.

Longhorn, F. (1991) 'A sensory science curriculum', in Ashdown, R., Carpenter, B. and Bovair, K. (Eds) *The Curriculum Challenge.* London: Falmer Press.

McConkey, R., McCormack, B. and Naughton, M. (1983a) *CARA Project Information Pack.* Dublin: St. Michael's House Research/Health Education Bureau.

McConkey, R. and McCormack, B. (1983b) *Breaking Barriers: Educating The Public About Disability*. London: Souvenir Press.

Marsh, C. (1988) 'Review of curriculum content and methods for severely handicapped students', *Australasian Journal of Special Education*, 11, 2, pp. 32-8.

Mittler, P. and Farrell, Peter (1987) 'Can children with severe learning difficulties be educated in ordinary schools?', *European Journal of Special Needs Education*, 2, pp. 221-36.

Moyles, J. R. (1989) *Just Playing? The Role and Status of Play in Early Childhood Education*. Buckingham: Open University Press.

National Curriculum Council (1990) *Curriculum Guidance 3: The Whole Curriculum*. York: NCC.

North West Mental Handicap Development Team (1989) *Overdale: Integrating Children with Severe Learning Difficulties into Mainstream Schools*. Team Report.

O'Grady, C. (1991) 'Caught in the Act?', *Times Education Supplement*, May 17.

Ouvry, C. (1987) *Educating Children with Profound Handicaps*. Kidderminster: BIMH.

Rix, B. (1990) 'The History of Mental Handicap and the Development of Mencap'. The 14th Stanley Segal lecture, University of Nottingham.

Sandler, A. and Robinson, R. (1981) 'Public attitudes and community acceptance of mentally retarded persons: A review', *Education and Training of The Mentally Retarded*, 16, pp. 97-103.

Sebba, J. (1983) 'Social interaction amongst pre-school handicapped and non-handicapped children', *Journal of Mental Deficiency*, 27, pp. 115-24.

Tomlinson, S. (1982) *A Sociology of Special Education*. London: Routledge & Kegan Paul.

Author Index

168

Subject Index